Prepared in cooperation with the North Carolina Department of Environment and Natural Resources, Division of Water Quality

I0438699

Water-Resources Data and Hydrogeologic Setting at the Raleigh Hydrogeologic Research Station, Wake County, North Carolina, 2005–2007

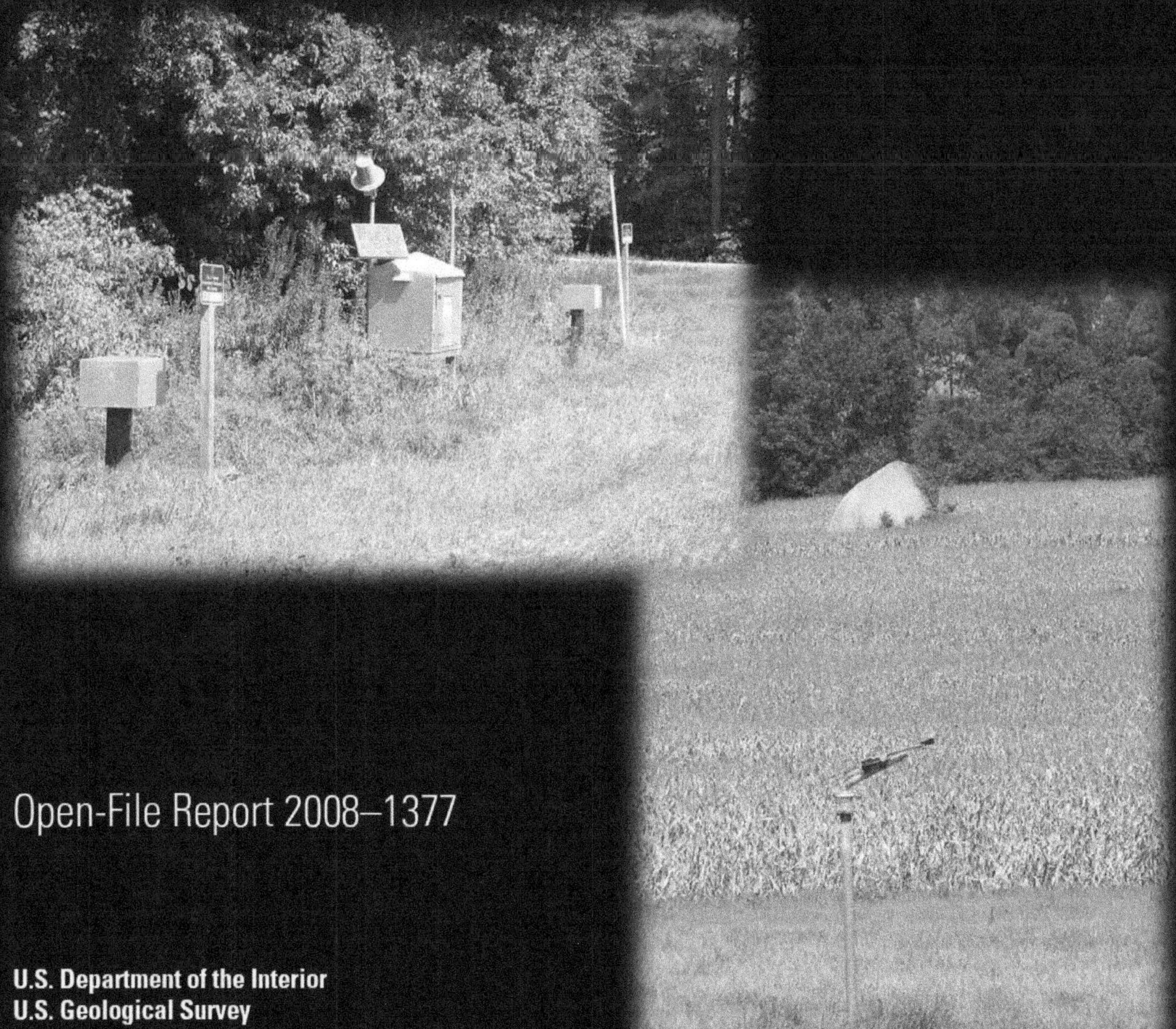

Open-File Report 2008–1377

U.S. Department of the Interior
U.S. Geological Survey

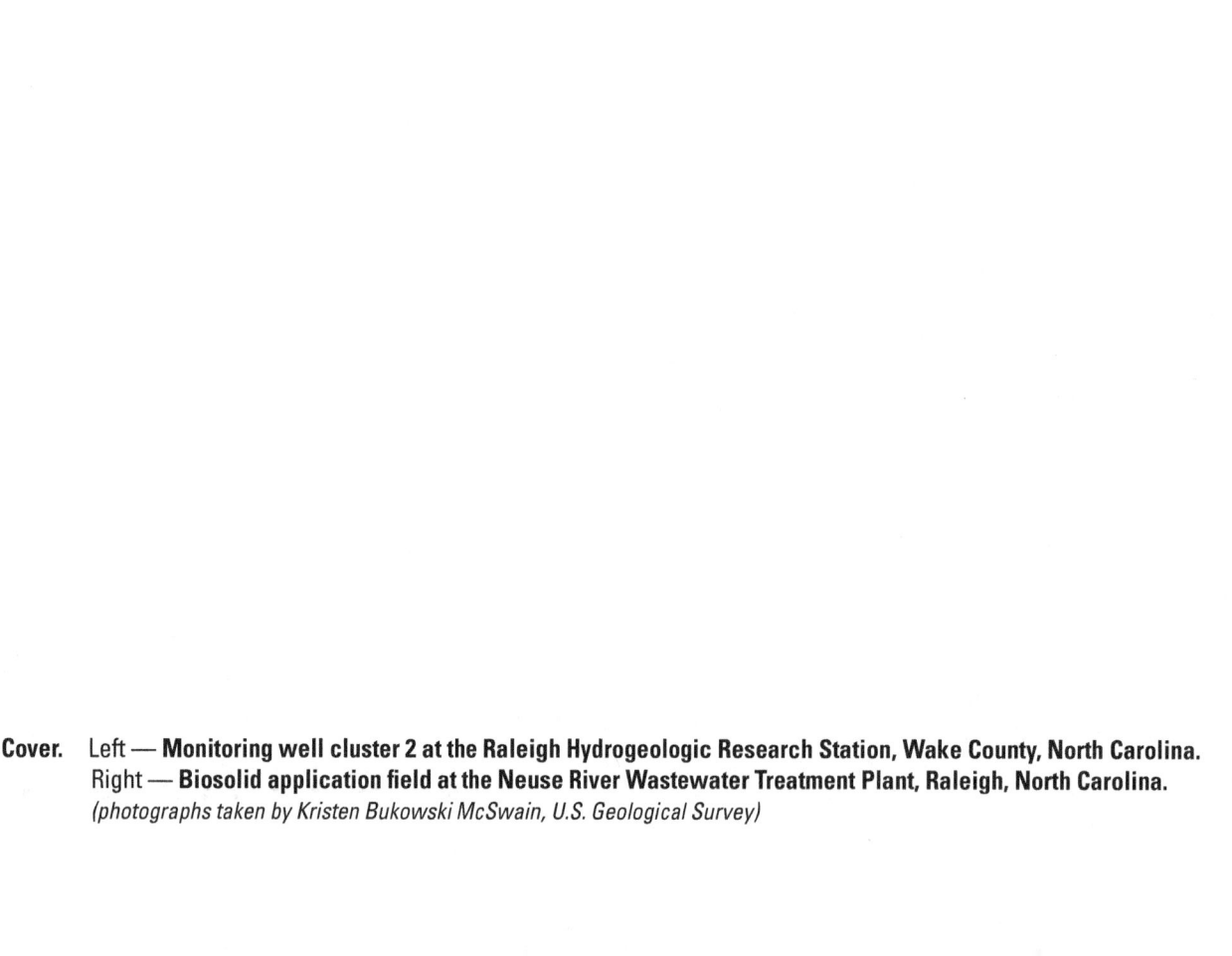

Cover. Left — **Monitoring well cluster 2 at the Raleigh Hydrogeologic Research Station, Wake County, North Carolina.**
Right — **Biosolid application field at the Neuse River Wastewater Treatment Plant, Raleigh, North Carolina.**
(photographs taken by Kristen Bukowski McSwain, U.S. Geological Survey)

Water-Resources Data and Hydrogeologic Setting at the Raleigh Hydrogeologic Research Station, Wake County, North Carolina, 2005–2007

By Kristen Bukowski McSwain, Richard E. Bolich, Melinda J. Chapman, and Brad A. Huffman

Prepared in cooperation with the North Carolina Department of Environment and Natural Resources, Division of Water Quality

Open-File Report 2008–1377

U.S. Department of the Interior
U.S. Geological Survey

U.S. Department of the Interior
DIRK KEMPTHORNE, Secretary

U.S. Geological Survey
Mark D. Myers, Director

U.S. Geological Survey, Reston, Virginia: 2009

For product and ordering information:
World Wide Web: http://www.usgs.gov/pubprod
Telephone: 1-888-ASK-USGS

For more information on the USGS—the Federal source for science about the Earth, its natural and living resources, natural hazards, and the environment:
World Wide Web: http://www.usgs.gov
Telephone: 1-888-ASK-USGS

Suggested citation:
McSwain, K.B., Bolich, R.E., Chapman, M.J., and Huffman, B.A., 2009, Water-resources data and hydrogeologic setting at the Raleigh hydrogeologic research station, Wake County, North Carolina, 2005–2007: U.S. Geological Survey Open-File Report 2008–1377, 48 p. (only online at http://pubs.water.usgs.gov/ofr2008-1377).

Contents

Figures

Tables

Conversion Factors

Inch/Pound to SI

Multiply	By	To obtain
Length		
inch (in.)	2.54	centimeter (cm)
inch (in.)	25.4	millimeter (mm)
foot (ft)	0.3048	meter (m)
mile (mi)	1.609	kilometer (km)
yard (yd)	0.9144	meter (m)
Area		
acre	4,047	square meter (m^2)
Volume		
quart (qt)	0.9464	liter (L)
gallon (gal)	3.785	liter (L)
million gallons (Mgal)	3,785	cubic meter (m^3)
Flow		
million gallons per day (Mgal/d)	0.04381	cubic meter per second (m^3/s)
Mass		
ton, short (2,000 lb)	0.9072	megagram (Mg)
ton per year (ton/yr)	0.9072	megagram per year (Mg/yr)
Hydraulic conductivity*		
foot per day (ft/d)	0.3048	meter per day (m/d)

SI to Inch/Pound

Multiply	By	To obtain
Length		
meter (m)	3.281	foot (ft)
Volume		
liter (L)	0.2642	gallon (gal)
Mass		
megagram (Mg)	1.102	ton, short (2,000 lb)
megagram per year (Mg/yr)	1.102	ton per year

Temperature in degrees Celsius (°C) may be converted to degrees Fahrenheit (°F) as follows:

$$°F = (1.8 × °C) + 32$$

Altitude, as used in this report, refers to distance above the vertical datum.

Vertical coordinate information is referenced to the North American Vertical Datum of 1988 (NAVD 88).

*Hydraulic conductivity: The standard unit for hydraulic conductivity is cubic foot per day per square foot of aquifer cross-sectional area [(ft^3/d)/ft^2]. In this report, the mathematically reduced form, feet per day (ft/d), is used for convenience.

Specific conductance is given in microsiemens per centimeter at 25 degrees Celsius (µS/cm at 25 °C).

Concentrations of chemical constituents in water are given either in milligrams per liter (mg/L) or micrograms per liter (µg/L).

Water-Resources Data and Hydrogeologic Setting at the Raleigh Hydrogeologic Research Station, Wake County, North Carolina, 2005–2007

By Kristen Bukowski McSwain, Richard E. Bolich,[1] Melinda J. Chapman, and Brad A. Huffman

Abstract

Water-resources data were collected to describe the hydrologic conditions at the Raleigh hydrogeologic research station, located in the Piedmont Physiographic Province of North Carolina. Data collected by the U.S. Geological Survey and the North Carolina Department of Environment and Natural Resources, Division of Water Quality, from May 2005 through September 2007 are presented in this report. Three well clusters and four piezometers were installed at the Raleigh hydrogeologic research station along an assumed flow path from recharge to discharge areas. Each well cluster includes four wells to monitor the regolith, transition zone, and shallow and deep bedrock. Borehole, surface, and waterborne geophysics were conducted to examine the lithology and physical properties of the bedrock and to determine the aerial extent of near vertical diabase dikes. Slug tests were conducted in the wells at each cluster to determine the hydraulic conductivity of the formation tapped by each well. Periodic water-level altitudes were measured in all wells and in four piezometers. Continuous hourly water levels were measured in wells for variable periods of time during the study, and a surface-water gage collected 15-minute stage data from April to June 2006. In October 2005 and April 2006, water-quality samples were collected from a tributary and in all wells at the Raleigh hydrogeologic research station. Continuous water-quality data were collected hourly in three wells from December 2005 through January 2007 and every 15 minutes in the tributary from May to June 2006. In August 2006, streambed temperatures and drive-point ground-water samples were collected across lines of section spanning the Neuse River.

[1]North Carolina Department of Environment and Natural Resources, Division of Water Quality, Aquifer Protection Section, Raleigh, North Carolina.

Introduction

The ground-water system in the piedmont and mountains of North Carolina is complex and susceptible to contamination. In order to better protect and manage the resource, the North Carolina legislature established the Piedmont and Mountains Resource Evaluation Program (PMREP) to ensure long-term availability, sustainability, and quality of ground water in this area of the State. In 1999, the U.S. Geological Survey (USGS) and the North Carolina Department of Environment and Natural Resources (NCDENR), Division of Water Quality (DWQ), began a multiyear cooperative study to measure ambient ground-water quality and describe the ground-water-flow systems at selected research stations in the Piedmont and Blue Ridge Physiographic Provinces of North Carolina (Daniel and Dahlen, 2002). A primary goal of the PMREP is the investigation of the vulnerability of the ground-water system to contamination (Chapman and others, 2005).

The PMREP was designed (Daniel and Dahlen, 2002) to be a 10-year intensive field investigation at research stations established in representative hydrogeologic settings across the State. To date (2008), 10 research stations have been selected for study in the Piedmont and Blue Ridge Physiographic Provinces (fig. 1), and wells have been installed at 8 of these research stations. Data collected as part of the PMREP provide information to refine the historical conceptual ground-water-flow models for the Piedmont and Blue Ridge Physiographic Provinces in North Carolina and the southeastern United States. The work conducted as part of this study supports the USGS mission of understanding processes in complex ground-water systems to aid water-resource managers in the protection and management of the resource.

Ground water in the Piedmont and Blue Ridge Provinces flows through geologic settings composed of metamorphic, igneous, and sedimentary (Triassic basins) rocks. Weathered regolith, composed of soil, residuum, saprolite, alluvium, and colluvium may overlie the fractured bedrock. Ground-water flow is complex, consisting of an interconnected but distinct two-component ground-water system, in which the regolith

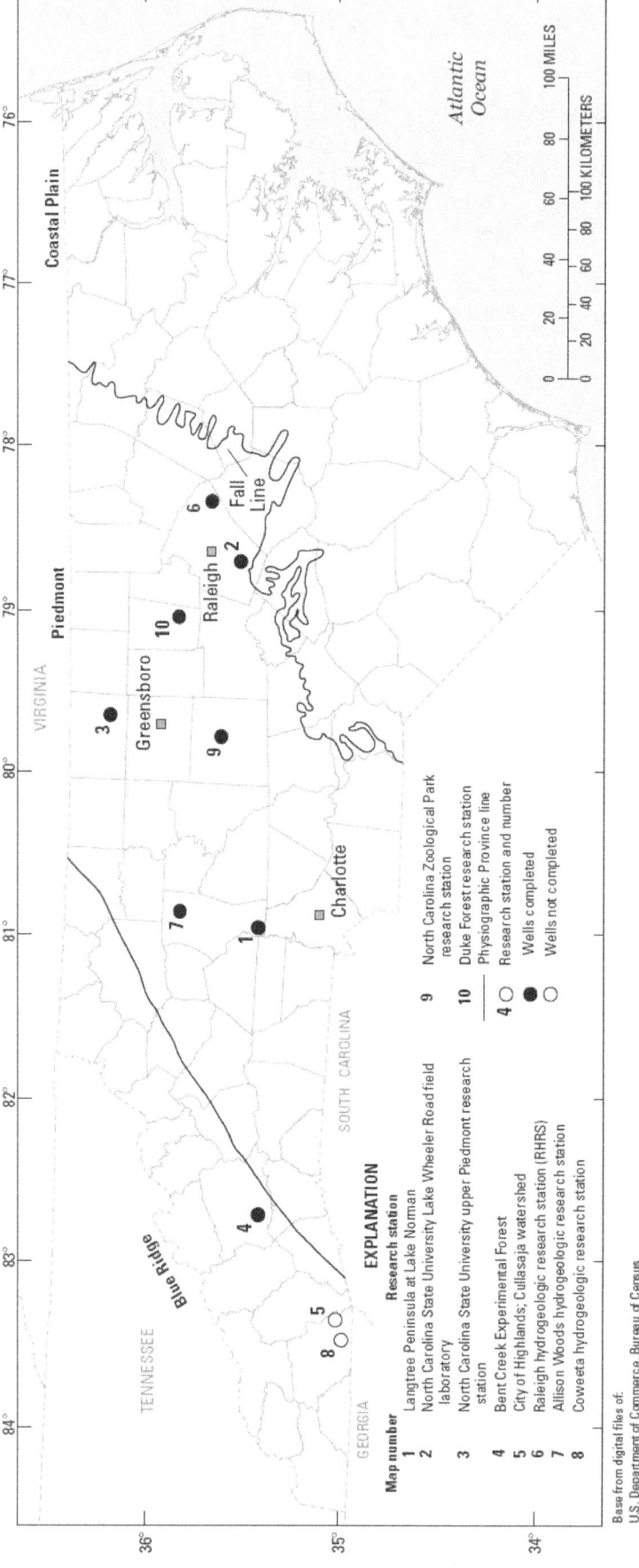

Figure 1.   Research stations selected for investigation as part of the cooperative U.S. Geological Survey and North Carolina Division of Water Quality Piedmont and Mountains Resource Evaluation Program in North Carolina.

provides storage for the underlying fractures in the bedrock (Heath, 1980). The PMREP investigation also includes a third component of the ground-water-flow system—the transition zone (fig. 2). The transition zone in the study area commonly is present between the regolith and bedrock (Harned and Daniel, 1992).

The location of the Raleigh hydrogeologic research station (RHRS; fig. 3) is representative of the igneous, felsic intrusive (IFI) hydrogeologic unit, which occurs in 5.4 percent of the Piedmont and Blue Ridge Provinces in North Carolina (Daniel and Dahlen, 2002). The RHRS was selected to evaluate the effects of felsic intrusive rocks with local shearing and jointing on ground-water quality, thickness and composition of the regolith, thickness and characteristics of the transition zone, and the development and characteristics of bedrock fractures.

Purpose and Scope

The purpose of this report is to summarize data collected from May 2005 through September 2007 at the RHRS, Wake County, North Carolina, and to describe the methods used to collect the data. Data compiled for this report include well-construction characteristics for 12 wells and 4 piezometers, periodic ground-water-level measurements for 12 wells and 4 piezometers, hourly ground-water-level measurements for 8 wells, continuous-stage measurements for 2 streams, continuous water-quality measurements for 3 wells and 1 stream, periodic water-quality measurements for 12 wells and 1 stream, and slug-test results for 12 wells. Streambed-temperature profiles were completed at 80 discrete locations, and water samples were collected at 47 locations beneath the Neuse River. Additionally, the geology and hydrogeology of the RHRS are summarized.

Description of the Study Area

The RHRS lies in the eastern part of the Piedmont Physiographic Province within the Raleigh Belt (litho-tectonic terrane; fig. 3) and is located about 9 miles east-southeast of Raleigh in Wake County, North Carolina. Based on observed rock outcrops and the bedrock-core samples from the RHRS, the study area is underlain by the Rolesville Batholith. The Rolesville Batholith is a granitic intrusion that is massive to

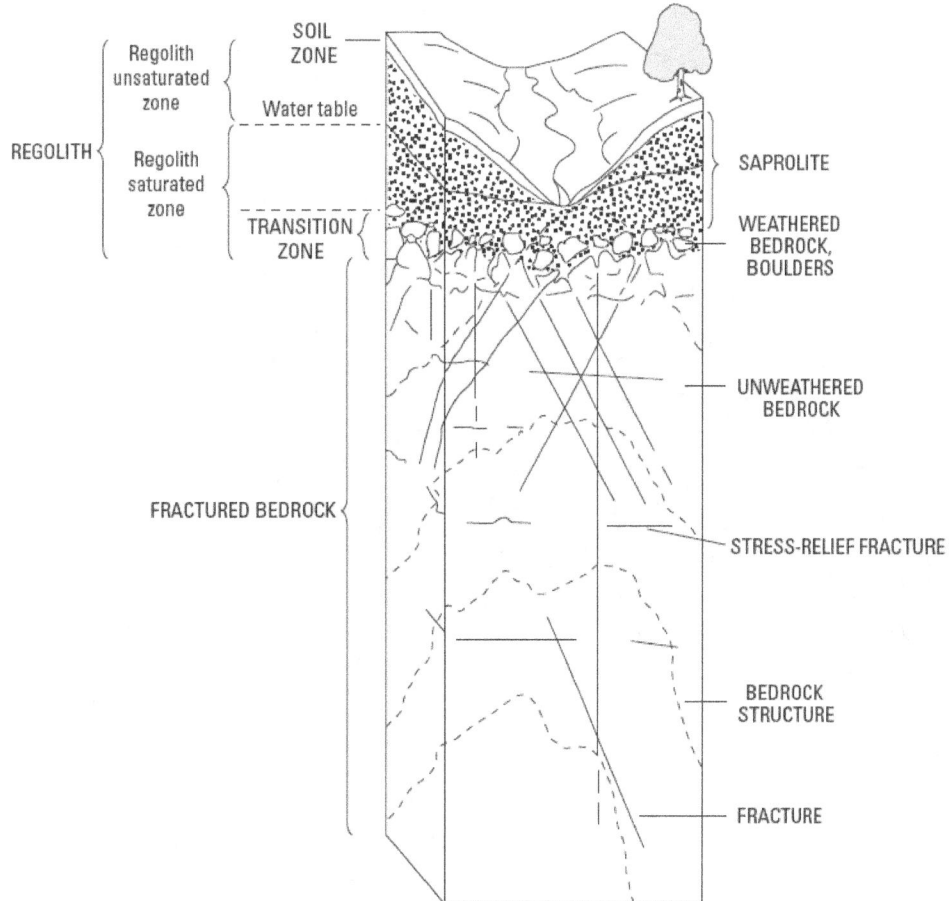

Figure 2. Conceptual components of the piedmont and mountains ground-water system in North Carolina (from Harned and Daniel, 1992).

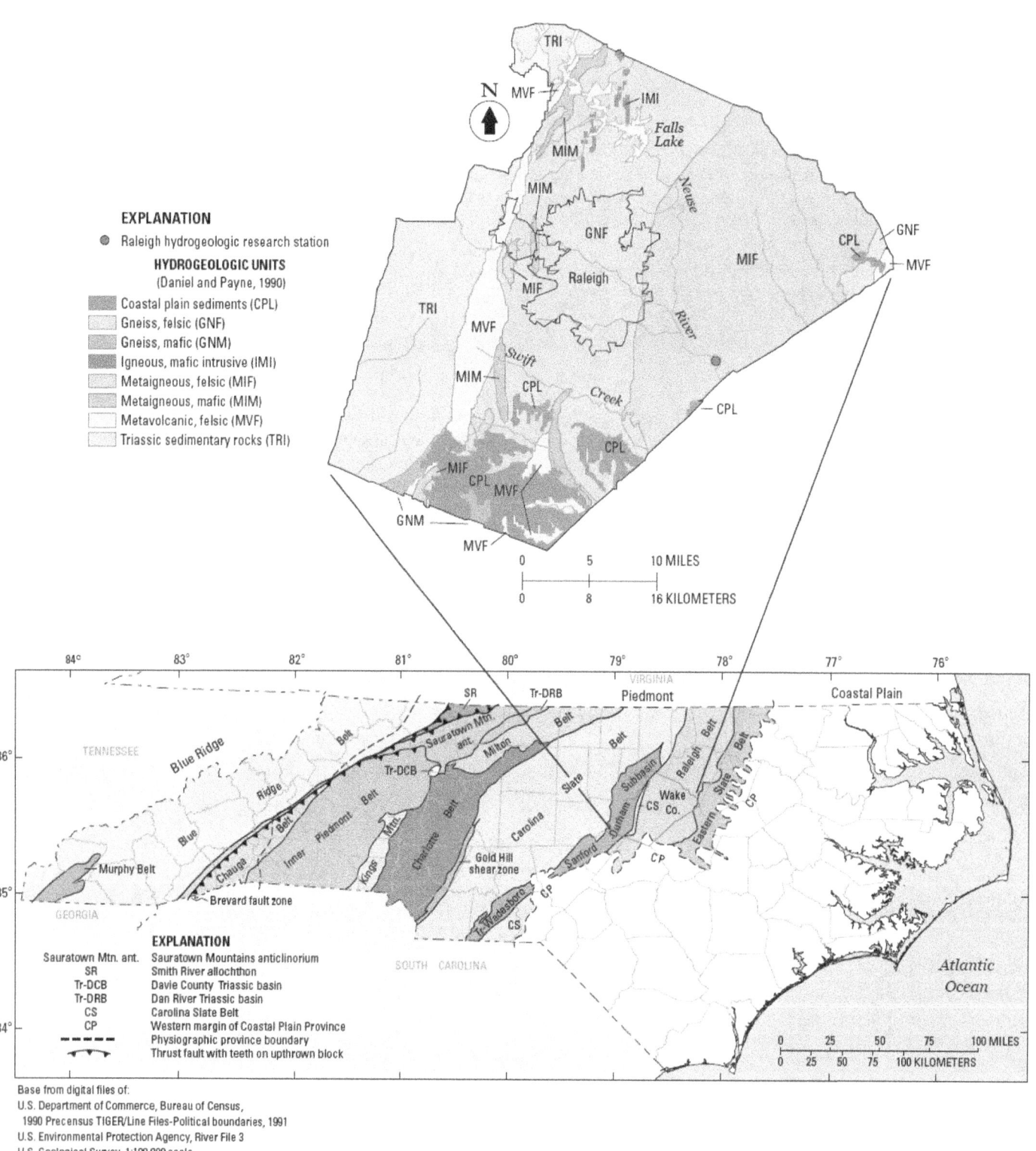

EXPLANATION
● Raleigh hydrogeologic research station

HYDROGEOLOGIC UNITS
(Daniel and Payne, 1990)
- Coastal plain sediments (CPL)
- Gneiss, felsic (GNF)
- Gneiss, mafic (GNM)
- Igneous, mafic intrusive (IMI)
- Metaigneous, felsic (MIF)
- Metaigneous, mafic (MIM)
- Metavolcanic, felsic (MVF)
- Triassic sedimentary rocks (TRI)

EXPLANATION
Sauratown Mtn. ant.	Sauratown Mountains anticlinorium
SR	Smith River allochthon
Tr-DCB	Davie County Triassic basin
Tr-DRB	Dan River Triassic basin
CS	Carolina Slate Belt
CP	Western margin of Coastal Plain Province
––––	Physiographic province boundary
⌒⌒⌒	Thrust fault with teeth on upthrown block

Base from digital files of:
U.S. Department of Commerce, Bureau of Census,
 1990 Precensus TIGER/Line Files-Political boundaries, 1991
U.S. Environmental Protection Agency, River File 3
U.S. Geological Survey, 1:100,000 scale

Figure 3   Locations of Raleigh hydrogeologic research station, hydrogeologic units in Wake County, and geologic belts delineated in the Piedmont Physiographic Province of North Carolina.

weakly foliated (Hibbard and others, 2002). Diabase dike intrusions (tabular basaltic bodies with a near vertical orientation) commonly are found in the Rolesville granite. The North Carolina geologic map (North Carolina Geological Survey, 1985) identifies a north-northwest striking diabase dike near the RHRS, although field reconnaissance of the RHRS study area revealed the presence of at least two additional diabase dikes that appear to strike roughly due north (Edward F. Stoddard, North Carolina State University, oral commun., January 26, 2005).

The RHRS occupies about 60 acres in close proximity to the City of Raleigh's Neuse River Wastewater Treatment Plant (NRWWTP) site (fig. 4). The NRWWTP treats about 45 million gallons per day (Mgal/d) of wastewater from Raleigh and other Wake County municipalities and has a current treatment capacity of 60 Mgal/d. From 1980 to 2002, the NRWWTP was permitted to dispose of 7,000 tons per year of treated biosolids onto 1,030 acres of fields that surround the plant, including the RHRS site (ENSR Consulting and Engineering, Inc., 2003).

The topography of the RHRS is characterized by gently rolling hills and moderately well-developed drainage features with land-surface altitudes in the study area ranging from approximately 150 feet (ft) near the Neuse River to 240 ft altitude in the southeast corner. Two unnamed tributaries to the east and west drain the study area and discharge to the north into the Neuse River (fig. 4).

Mean annual rainfall for the Wake County area is about 46 inches. The greatest precipitation normally occurs in the summer, and July is the wettest month. The driest season generally is autumn, and November generally is the driest month. Hurricanes affect North Carolina about twice in an average year (State Climate Office of North Carolina, 2007); as recently as June 2006, the area was affected by tropical storm Alberto. During 2007, the study area received about 35 inches of rain and was affected by drought conditions.

In 2005, the population of Wake County was about 748,000 people, and the total ground-water use was estimated to be about 19.3 Mgal/d (U.S. Geological Survey, 2008). Although a major metropolitan area (Raleigh) lies within Wake County, about 110,000 county residents (about 14 percent) use wells as their primary source of drinking water (U.S. Geological Survey, 2008), including the majority of residents in the area surrounding the RHRS. Most of the land use in Wake County is urban and suburban; as a result, many contaminant-release incidents are reported to the DWQ (Lori K. Skidmore, North Carolina Division of Water Quality, oral commun., December 3, 2007).

Well and Surface-Water Station Numbering System

Wells and surface-water stations monitored by the USGS are given unique identification numbers based on geographic location. A latitude-longitude system is used for wells and drive points, and a downstream-order system is used for surface-water stations. The latitude and longitude of each well cluster and the surface-water station at the RHRS were determined by using a differential global positioning system (DGPS) receiver and are considered accurate to within a few feet (Chapman and others, 2005).

Wells were assigned a 15-digit site number based on latitude and longitude. The latitude and longitude constitute the first 13 digits, respectively, and are followed by a 2-digit sequence number used to distinguish among wells clustered closely together. Each well in a cluster has the same site-identification number except for the last two digits. Typically, the assigned sequence numbers begin with 01 for the shallowest well and progress with well depth at each cluster. Thus, the deeper the well, the higher the sequence number (Chapman and others, 2005).

In addition to the standard USGS well-numbering system, the wells in this study also were assigned a local identifier, which consists of a two-letter North Carolina county code followed by a three-digit sequence number. For example, wells in Wake County are identified by the prefix "WK" followed by three numbers that are assigned sequentially. The station name includes the site identifier (Raleigh research station [RS]), well descriptor, and number. The well descriptors used in this study are WC for monitoring well and PZ for piezometer. Following the well descriptor is a cluster number and a letter, which indicates the aquifer section or zone that is being monitored: "S" for shallow zone (regolith), "I" for intermediate or transition zone, and "D" for deeper zone (bedrock). For example, well WC-1S is a monitoring well in cluster 1 and is completed in the shallow regolith zone.

The drive-point locations in this study were assigned a 15-digit site number based on the latitude and longitude of the transect anchor point on the right bank (facing downstream) of the Neuse River. The latitude and longitude constitute the first 13 digits, respectively, and are followed by a 2-digit sequence number used to distinguish between drive-point locations following the same line of transect. Each drive point in a transect has the same site identification number except for the last two digits, which incrementally increase with distance along the transect. Thus, the farther away a drive point is along the line of section from the first point in the transect, the higher the sequence number. The station name includes the site identifier (Raleigh RS), the transect identifier (F–F'), and the distance, in feet, from the right bank of the Neuse River where the drive point was inserted.

The downstream order number or station number assigned to a surface-water station is based on the location of the station in the downstream direction along the main stem of the stream. The first 2 digits of the 8- to 10-digit station number identify the hydrologic unit (U.S. Geological Survey, 1974, 1975) used by the USGS to designate the major drainage system. The next six digits indicate the downstream order within the major drainage system. An additional two-digit number is added at the end of the station number in areas of high station density (Chapman and others, 2005).

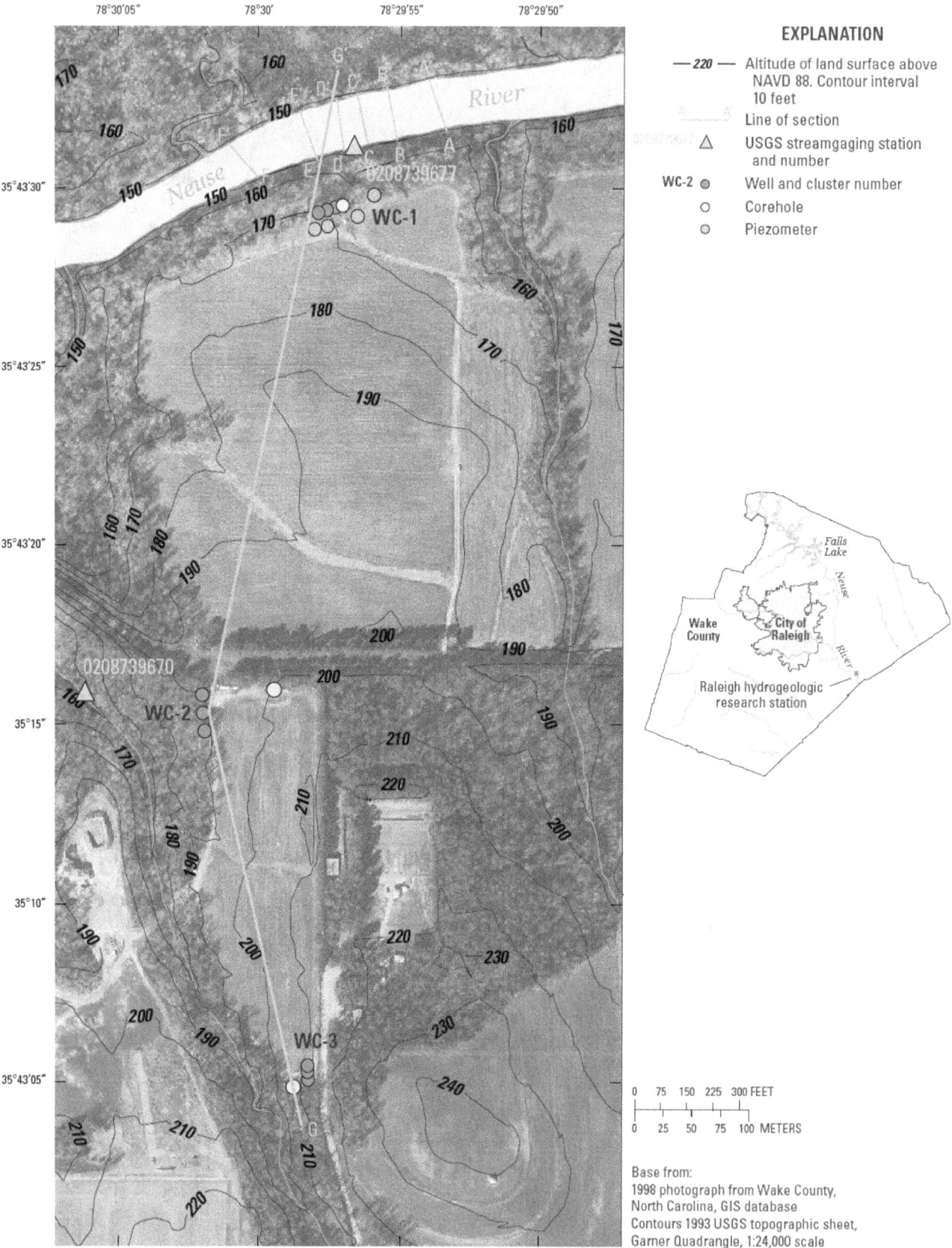

Figure 4.   Aerial photograph of the Raleigh hydrogeologic research station, Wake County, North Carolina, overlaid with topographic features showing locations of well clusters, streamgages, and lines of section.

Methods of Data Collection

The data-collection methods that were used in the study are summarized in this section of the report. The standard operating procedures (SOP) are procedures of the PMREP (Richard E. Bolich, North Carolina Department of Water Quality, written commun., 2008).

Research Stations

Research stations consisting of a transect of monitoring-well clusters were installed in representative hydrogeologic settings, parallel to an assumed flow path within a conceptual "slope-aquifer" system, from recharge (higher elevation, such as hilltops) to discharge areas (lower elevations, such as stream valleys), as described by LeGrand (2004). Criteria for determining well-cluster locations at the RHRS included topographic position, accessibility, and site boundaries. A generalized hydrogeologic transect was constructed from the presumed recharge area at WC-3 to the presumed discharge area at WC-1 (fig. 5). Each well cluster is designed to monitor separate zones in the ground-water system, including the shallow regolith, transition zone, and deep bedrock (Chapman and others, 2005).

Well Construction

A continuous soil and bedrock core was collected using wire-line coring methods at each of the monitoring-well cluster locations. The coreholes provided continuous samples resulting in soil-to-bedrock profiles at each well cluster that were used to determine construction requirements for the monitoring wells. Upon completion of coring, each corehole was converted to a bedrock monitoring well and designated as WC-1CH, WC-2CH, and WC-3CH, respectively. Well-construction details for each corehole are given in table 1; detailed core descriptions are given in appendixes 1–3. After coring was completed, three representative rock samples from each corehole (nine samples total) were selected for whole-rock analyses for major elements. Whole-rock analyses were conducted by the USGS Mineral Resources team in Denver, CO, using methods described in Taggart (2002).

Shallow, intermediate, and deep monitoring wells at the RHRS were constructed by using hollow-stem auger, mud-rotary, and air-rotary drilling methods. Both mud-rotary and hollow-stem auger drilling methods were used to construct wells in the regolith ("S"), the transition zone ("I"), and the piezometers ("PZ"). The bedrock ("D") wells were constructed by using a combination of mud-rotary drilling to set the casing and air-rotary drilling to bore the open-hole section of the bedrock. Specific well-construction techniques are described in Chapman and others (2005).

During this investigation, 12 wells (4 at each well cluster) were installed to monitor three separate zones in the ground-water system at the RHRS. Cross section G–G' was constructed along a transect from well cluster WC-1 to WC-3 (fig. 5). Four piezometers were installed near WC-1 to provide aquifer-test data and to obtain detailed data to define the two-dimensional ground-water flow in the regolith in this area.

Geophysics

Borehole geophysical logs were collected at each cluster in the wells that are completed with open boreholes (the "D" and "CH" wells). Traditional borehole geophysical logs (caliper; natural gamma; short-normal, long-normal, and lateral resistivities; and fluid temperature and resistivity) were collected after well completion, along with electromagnetic flowmeter and optical televiewer (OTV) logs (Keys, 1990). Flowmeter logging was conducted under ambient and(or) stressed (pumped at a constant rate) conditions. The OTV data enable the identification of lithology type (felsic or mafic), rock-foliation orientation, and fracture orientation. The fracture orientation data are shown in tadpole plots where dip angle is plotted as a circle and azimuth direction is plotted as a line segment. The OTV data presented in this report have been corrected for magnetic declination and borehole deviation (azimuth and inclination angle). All geophysical logs collected and reported here are referenced to feet below land surface (Chapman and others, 2005).

A portable proton procession magnetometer was used to conduct a magnetic field survey along the bank of the Neuse River and in the study area. The magnetometer measures the strength of the magnetic field in the near vicinity of the instrument. A change in the magnitude of the magnetic field around the instrument can mean a change in shallow subsurface rock type, particularly in deposits of iron-rich rocks (Rubin and Hubbard, 2005).

Waterborne continuous resistivity profiling was conducted on the Neuse River in the vicinity of the study area to measure the apparent resistivity distribution of the sediments, bedrock, and pore-water fluid beneath the streambed. Continuous resistivity profiling was conducted following methods similar to those outlined in Day-Lewis and others (2006). Apparent resistivity data were collected using an 8-channel resistivity system and an electrode streamer with 11 electrodes at a 5-meter (16.4 ft) spacing. The first two electrodes in the streamer inject current through the water column and into the ground while the nine trailing electrodes simultaneously measure eight voltage potentials (the potential difference between two electrodes). These apparent resistivity data can be inverted to develop a geomodel of the subsurface structure and stratigraphy in terms of its electrical properties (Snyder and Wightman, 2002).

Monitoring

Monitoring of water levels, stream stage, and water quality was conducted at selected RHRS sites for both ground water and surface water. Measurements were collected

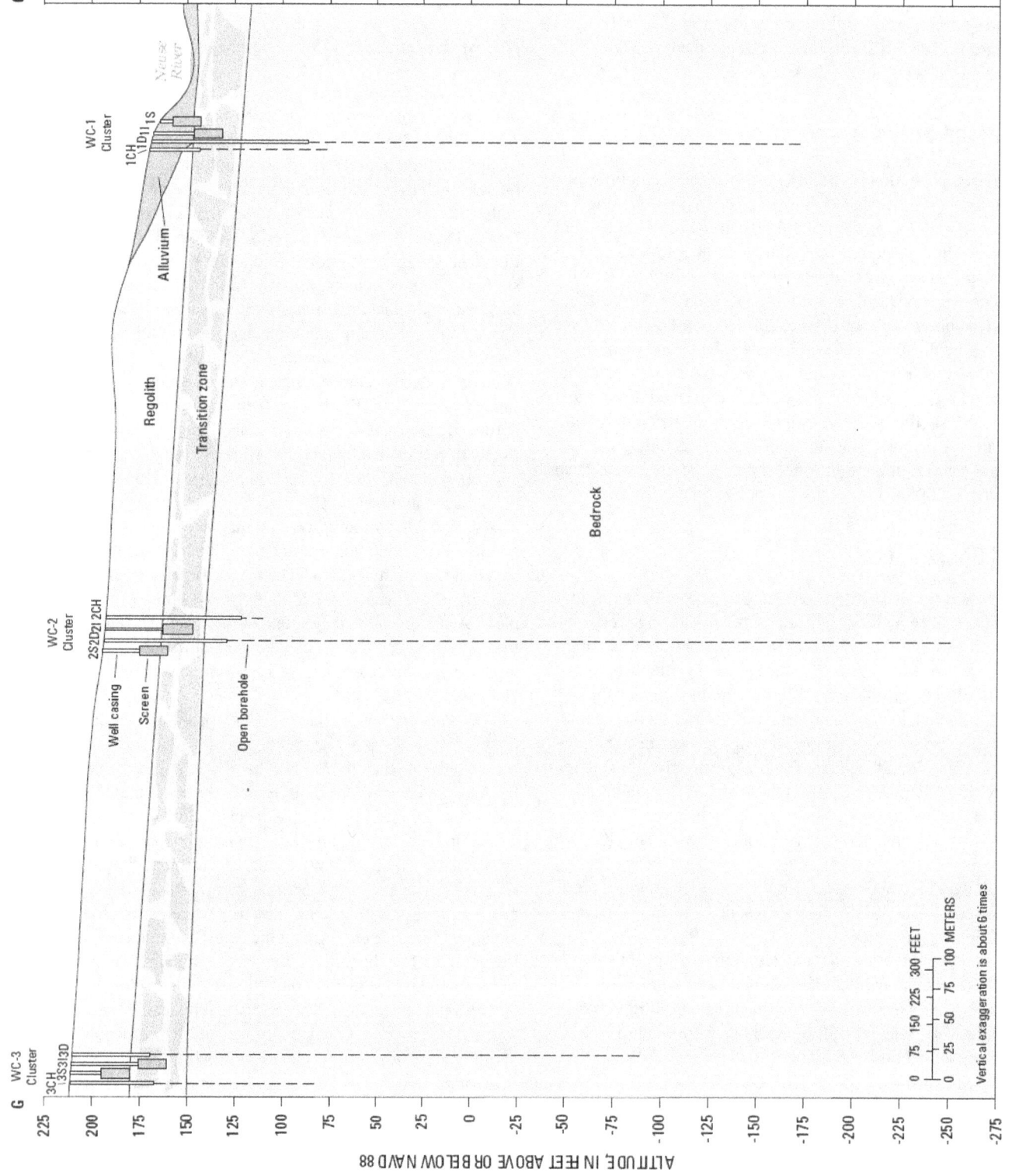

Figure 5.   Generalized hydrogeologic cross section G–G′ along the well transects at the Raleigh hydrogeologic research station, North Carolina.

Table 1.   Characteristics of the monitoring wells and the surface-water sites at the Raleigh hydrogeologic research station, Wake County, North Carolina.

[ddmmss.ss, degrees, minutes, seconds; NAVD 88, North American Vertical Datum of 1988; WK, Wake County; RS, research station; WC, well cluster; S, shallow regolith; I, intermediate zone regolith; D, deep; CH, core hole; PZ, piezometer; PVC, Schedule 40 polyvinyl chloride casing; Galv. steel, galvanized steel; R, regolith; T, transition zone; B, bedrock; SW, surface-water site; unk, unknown; na, not applicable; SR, secondary road]

Site identification	Station name	Latitude ddmmss.ss	Longitude ddmmss.ss	Construction date	Land-surface altitude (feet above NAVD 88)	Top of casing altitude (feet above NAVD 88)	Casing material	Casing diameter (inches)	Screened interval or open borehole interval (feet below land surface) from	to	Screen type	Zone monitored
354328078295701	WK-328 Raleigh RS WC-1S	354328.83	782957.83	3/30/2005	171.24	173.74	PVC	4	13	28	0.01 in. slotted PVC	R
354328078295702	WK-329 Raleigh RS WC-1I	354328.86	782957.66	3/29/2005	170.90	173.62	PVC	4	24	39	0.01 in. slotted PVC	T
354328078295703	WK-330 Raleigh RS WC-1D	354328.95	782957.3	4/6/2005	169.27	172.07	Galv. steel	6	82	342	Open hole	B
354328078295704	WK-331 Raleigh RS WC-1CH	354329.12	782956.93	1/12/2005	165.48	167.83	Galv. steel	6	21	90	Open hole	B
354328078295705	WK-369 Raleigh RS PZ-1	354328.38	782958.2	2/14/2005	172.23	174.73	PVC	1	14.5	24.5	0.01 in. slotted PVC	R
354328078295706	WK-370 Raleigh RS PZ-2	354328.52	782957.65	2/15/2005	171.37	173.87	PVC	1	17.5	27.5	0.01 in. slotted PVC	R
354328078295707	WK-371 Raleigh RS PZ-3	354328.74	782956.7	2/15/2005	165.32	167.82	PVC	1	19	29	0.01 in. slotted PVC	R
354328078295708	WK-372 Raleigh RS PZ-4	354329.33	782956.07	2/15/2005	166.94	169.44	PVC	1	16	26	0.01 in. slotted PVC	R
354315078300101	WK-332 Raleigh RS WC-2S	354314.77	783001.87	3/31/2005	189.64	192.33	PVC	4	13.5	28.5	0.01 in. slotted PVC	R
354315078300102	WK-333 Raleigh RS WC-2I	354315.74	783001.92	4/5/2005	189.95	192.45	PVC	4	27	42	0.01 in. slotted PVC	T
354315078300103	WK-334 Raleigh RS WC-2D	354315.28	783001.91	2/17/2005	188.49	191.23	Galv. steel	6	59	440	Open hole	B
354315078300104	WK-335 Raleigh RS WC-2CH	354316.1	782959.35	2/8/2005	199.50	202.22	PVC	4	70	85	0.01 in. slotted PVC	B
354305078295801	WK-336 Raleigh RS WC-3S	354305.41	782958.16	2/15/2005	209.73	212.42	PVC	4	13.5	28.5	0.01 in. slotted PVC	R
354305078295802	WK-337 Raleigh RS WC-3I	354305.59	782958.14	2/9/2005	210.27	212.96	PVC	4	34	49	0.01 in. slotted PVC	T
354305078295803	WK-338 Raleigh RS WC-3D	354305.72	782958.13	1/13/2005	209.83	212.53	Galv. steel	6	40	300	Open hole	B
354305078295804	WK-339 Raleigh RS WC-3CH	354305.24	782958.67	12/14/2005	206.27	208.69	PVC	4	40	125	Open hole	B
0208739670	Neuse River tributary near Auburn, NC	354316.17	783006.24	4/15/2006	unk.	na	na	na	na	na	na	SW
0208739677	Neuse River below SR2555 near Auburn, NC	354330.61	782956.52	2/28/2006	142.65	na	na	na	na	na	na	SW
02087500	Neuse River near Clayton	353850	782419	8/1/1927	128.41	na	na	na	na	na	na	SW

periodically or on a continuous basis. The periods of record for each type of data collection are described in table 2. In this report, ground-water-level data are presented in feet above the North American Vertical Datum of 1988 (NAVD 88).

Periodic Water-Level Measurements

Periodic ground-water levels were measured monthly at all of the wells at the RHRS to identify seasonal ground-water trends in each of the three monitored zones (regolith, transition zone, and fractured bedrock) and to qualitatively describe vertical hydraulic gradients between wells in each cluster. Measurements were made using either a steel tape or an electric water-level tape from a specified measuring point (MP) on top of the well casing. The MP and land surface at each well were surveyed, and the altitudes were related to a locally established benchmark to determine the MP and water-level altitude above NAVD 88. Water levels were recorded in feet below land surface and entered into the USGS Ground Water Site Inventory (GWSI) database. Water-level data are available online (U.S. Geological Survey, 2006b) and in USGS North Carolina Water Science Center annual data reports available online (U.S. Geological Survey, 2007). Periodic ground-water levels were collected following methods described in Garber and Koopman (1968).

Continuous Monitoring

Ground-water levels were measured hourly at selected sites by using a submersible pressure transducer. Stream stage was measured every 15 minutes by using a submersible pressure transducer or shaft encoder. Water-quality measurements were obtained hourly in selected wells and every 15 minutes at the surface-water sites by using a multiparameter water-quality probe. All of the water-quality probes and pressure transducers were connected to a data-collection platform (DCP) where the data were recorded. Each DCP was powered by a 12-volt battery and equipped with a solar panel to recharge the battery, housed in a sealed aluminum shelter, and grounded with copper wire for surge and lightning protection. The wiring was protected by conduit and buried 6–12 inches below the ground.

Continuous monitoring data are collected at a specified interval (hourly or every 15-minutes) and transmitted by satellite every 4 hours to a USGS database for processing. Data are accessible in the USGS National Water Information System (NWIS) database (U.S. Geological Survey, 2006c). Continuous ground-water and water-quality data collected at the RHRS during water year 2006 are published in the USGS annual data report (U.S. Geological Survey, 2007).

At the RHRS, a continuous ground-water-level recording network was established in well clusters WC-2 (four wells) and WC-1 (three wells). The pressure transducers were field checked periodically and corrected to measurements made with a steel or electric tape to ensure accurate reading following methods described in Freeman and others (2004). Water-level data are stored in NWIS relative to feet below land surface.

Continuous water quality was monitored at the RHRS in three wells at WC-2 and at one surface-water site. Water-quality data were collected hourly in the wells and at 15-minute intervals at the surface-water sites using multiparameter probes. The water-quality properties measured were water temperature, dissolved oxygen (DO), pH, and specific conductance (SC). The water-quality probes were inspected, cleaned, and calibrated according to USGS guidelines (Wagner and others, 2006).

Slug Tests

Rising and falling slug tests were performed on the 12 wells installed at the RHRS to measure aquifer hydraulic conductivity. Either solid polyvinyl chloride (PVC) slugs or PVC bailers were used to displace water in the wells. The solid slug or bailer was rinsed with distilled water before use in each well. A submersible pressure transducer with an integrated electronic data logger was used to measure water-level fluctuations during each test. Water-level data recorded on the transducer data logger were verified by manual water-level measurements.

When the solid slug was used, both falling (slug in) and rising (slug out) head data were analyzed. When a bailer was used, only rising head data were analyzed. The falling head slug test measured the rate at which water levels returned to static conditions after the introduction of the solid slug. The rising head test measured the recovery of water levels to static conditions after the slug was removed. Efforts were made to avoid splashing effects during the introduction of the slug below the water level. The tests were terminated after water levels recovered to within 95 percent of the pre-test static water level.

The slug-test data were analyzed using the Bouwer and Rice (1976) method, which accounts for partial penetration effects and changing aquifer thickness (water-table conditions). A basic assumption of this analytical method is that the aquifer is representative of a porous medium and is considered isotropic, with no directional variation in hydraulic properties in the zone being tested. Additional assumptions are that the effects of elastic storage can be neglected and that the position of the water table does not change during the slug test (Butler, 1998). Spreadsheets developed by Halford and Kuniansky (2002) were used for analytical interpretations of slug-test data.

Water-Quality Sampling

Water-quality samples were collected from each monitoring well at each cluster and a nearby stream by following standard USGS protocols outlined in U.S. Geological Survey (2006a). Sampling methods included the use of submersible pumps and peristaltic pumps. Pumping rate, drawdown, and water-quality properties (pH, SC, DO, and temperature) were monitored and documented during well purging. Water-quality

Table 2.   Periods of data collection for ground-water levels, surface-water stage, and water-quality measurements in wells and the Neuse River tributary near Auburn, North Carolina, at the Raleigh hydrogeologic research station, Wake County, North Carolina.

[WC, well cluster; S, shallow regolith; I, intermediate zone regolith; D, deep; CH, core hole; PZ, piezometer; na, not available; SR, secondary road]

Station name	Water level/stage		Water-quality continuous data (collected hourly for wells and every 15 minutes for surface water)
	Periodic data (monthly)	Continuous data (collected hourly for wells and every 15 minutes for surface water)	
WC-1S	05/2005 to 09/2007	05/2005 to 09/2007	na
WC-1I	05/2005 to 09/2007	05/2005 to 09/2007	na
WC-1D	05/2005 to 09/2007	05/2005 to 08/2005	na
WC-1CH	05/2005 to 09/2007	05/2005 to 06/2007	na
PZ-1	02/2006 to 07/2006	na	na
PZ-2	02/2006 to 07/2006	na	na
PZ-3	02/2006 to 07/2006	na	na
PZ-4	02/2006 to 07/2006	na	na
WC-2S	05/2005 to 09/2007	12/2005 to 09/2007	12/2005 to 01/2007
WC-2I	05/2005 to 09/2007	12/2005 to 09/2007	12/2005 to 01/2007
WC-2D	05/2005 to 09/2007	12/2005 to 09/2007	12/2005 to 01/2007
WC-2CH	05/2005 to 09/2007	06/2006 to 01/2007	na
WC-3S	05/2005 to 09/2007	na	na
WC-3I	05/2005 to 09/2007	na	na
WC-3D	05/2005 to 09/2007	na	na
WC-3CH	05/2005 to 09/2007	na	na
Neuse River tribuary near Auburn, NC (0208739670)	na	na	05/2005 to 06/2006
Neuse River below SR2555 near Auburn, NC (0208739677)	na	04/2006 to 06/2006	na
Neuse River near Clayton (02087500)	na	05/2005 to 09/2007	na

properties were measured continuously using a multiparameter water-quality instrument and flowthrough chamber connected to the pump discharge line. Prior to sample collection, at least three well volumes of ground water were removed from the 4-inch diameter shallow screened wells tapping the regolith and transition zone. For the deeper 6-inch diameter open-borehole bedrock wells, extracting three well volumes of ground water prior to sample collection was impractical when using a submersible sampling pump. For these wells, a minimum of one volume of casing water was removed and water-quality properties were allowed to stabilize prior to sample collection. Pump intakes were placed near the more dominant fracture zones (Chapman and others, 2005).

A Multifunction Bedrock-Aquifer Transportable Testing Tool (BAT[3]) was used in one sampling event to collect water-quality samples in the open boreholes at the RHRS. The BAT[3] allows discrete intervals of a borehole to be isolated hydraulically for geochemical sampling by using two inflatable packers that seal against the borehole wall. The spacing between the two packers defines the test interval in the borehole. The equipment is configured with a submersible pump located between the packers to withdraw water from the test interval in order to collect water-quality samples. The length of the test interval and the depth at which water-quality samples were collected were determined based on the location of the fractures intersecting the borehole, as identified in the borehole geophysical logs. A complete discussion of the down-hole components of the BAT[3] and its operation is given in Shapiro (2001).

Quality-assurance and quality-control (QA/QC) activities included the collection of blank and replicate samples for chemical analysis. Field QA/QC samples were collected to ensure sampling data accuracy (lack of bias) and precision. Field blanks were prepared onsite by processing blank water through the same equipment used to collect and process the field samples. Field replicate samples were collected to ensure data precision. QA/QC data are stored at the USGS North Carolina Water Science Center in Raleigh and are available upon request.

The water-quality constituents analyzed include major ions, nutrients, metals, radon 222 (gas), radiochemicals, and dissolved gases. Of these, only samples for major ions and nutrients were collected during each sampling event. Water samples for all other constituents were collected intermittently or one time only. Sampling locations, constituents, and sampling dates for water-quality sample collection are listed in table 3.

Water samples were analyzed by the USGS National Water Quality Laboratory (NWQL) in Denver, CO, for inorganic ions, nutrients, radon 222 (gas), wastewater compounds, trace metals, and pharmaceuticals by using methods outlined in Fishman (1993). Bacteria samples were processed locally in the USGS North Carolina Water Science Center laboratory using methods described in U.S. Geological Survey (2006a). Tritium, dissolved gases, and chlorofluorocarbon (CFC) samples were analyzed at the USGS Chlorofluorocar-

bon Laboratory in Reston, VA, as described in Busenberg and Plummer (1992), and helium samples were analyzed at the Noble Gas Laboratory of Lamont-Doherty Earth Observatory of Columbia University in New York, NY.

Analytical results of the water-quality sampling data are available online (U.S. Geological Survey, 2006c) and in USGS annual data reports (U.S. Geological Survey, 2007). Some samples from bedrock well WC-1D may have been affected by grout migration and were not published because of elevated pH, alkalinity, calcium, and sulfate concentrations. Analytical results of the water-quality sampling data analyzed by the USGS Chlorofluorocarbon Laboratory and the Noble Gas Laboratory are stored at the USGS North Carolina Water Science Center in Raleigh and are available upon request.

Statistical Analysis of Water-Quality Data

The statistical and geochemical variability in the periodic water-quality data are summarized in box plots, Piper diagrams, and Stiff diagrams. Prior to the statistical analysis, a quality-assurance check was conducted on the water-quality data. A mass balance with less than 10-percent difference for the major cations and anions was considered acceptable, and only these data were included in the statistical analyses (U.S. Geological Survey, 1992).

Box plots statistically categorize data, identify outliers, and can be an effective means of comparing values between data sets. The box encompasses the interval between the first and third quartiles, also known as the interquartile range. The median is represented by a horizontal line within the rectangular box. The minimum and maximum values of the data set are represented by a whisker attached to a vertical line drawn from the first and third quartiles, respectively, to those values (Sincich, 1993).

Water-quality data can be compared by using Piper trilinear diagrams (Piper, 1953) and Stiff diagrams (Stiff, 1951). In a Piper diagram, the percentages of cations are plotted in the left trilinear diagram, and the percentages of anions are plotted in the right trilinear diagram. The diamond shaped middle diagram plots the cations and anions together. Stiff diagrams show the dominant milliequivalent-per-liter concentrations of anions and cations in the collected samples. In this report, water-quality data are grouped for display by surface water and ground-water-system zone (regolith, transition zone, and bedrock).

Neuse River Ground-Water and Surface-Water Interaction

Because of the close proximity of the Neuse River to the study site, information about the degree of hydraulic connection between the aquifer and the overlying river is important. At the RHRS, temperature measurements and drive-point water-quality samples were collected over a 3-day period in August 2006 in the riverbed to better understand the

Table 3. Sampling locations, constituents, and sampling dates for water-quality samples collected at the Raleigh hydrogeologic research station, Wake County, North Carolina.

[ft BLS, feet below land surface; CFC, chlorofluorocarbon; WC, well cluster; I, intermediate zone regolith; D, deep; CH, core hole; na, not applicable; --, not sampled]

Site identification number	Station name	Packer interval sampled (ft BLS)	Bacteria	Major inorganic ions	Nutrients	CFC	Tritium	Helium	Dissolved gases	Radon	Waste-water compounds	Trace metals	Pharma-ceuticals
354328078295701	WC-1S	na	10/2005	10/2005 04/2006	10/2005 04/2006	04/2006	04/2006	--	--	--	--	--	--
354328078295702	WC-1I	na	10/2005	10/2005 04/2006	10/2005 04/2006	04/2006	04/2006	04/2006	04/2006	--	--	--	--
354328078295703	WC-1D	na	10/2005	10/2005	10/2005 04/2006 09/2007	--	04/2006	04/2006	--	09/2007	--	--	--
354328078295704	WC-1CH	na	10/2005	10/2005 04/2006	10/2005 04/2006	04/2006	04/2006	04/2006	04/2006	09/2007	--	--	--
354315078300101	WC-2S	na	10/2005	10/2005 12/2005 04/2006	10/2005 12/2005 04/2006 09/2007	04/2006	04/2006	04/2006	04/2006	09/2007	12/2005	12/2005	12/2005
354315078300102	WC-2I	na	10/2005	10/2005 04/2006	10/2005 04/2006 09/2007	04/2006	04/2006	04/2006	04/2006	09/2007	--	--	--
354315078300103	WC-2D	na	10/2005	10/2005	10/2005 09/2007	--	--	--	--	09/2007	--	--	--
354315078300103	WC-2D	59–77	--	03/2006	03/2006	03/2006	03/2006	--	03/2006	--	--	--	--
354315078300103	WC-2D	244–260	--	03/2006	03/2006	03/2006	03/2006	--	03/2006	--	--	--	--
354315078300104	WC-2CH	na	10/2005	10/2005	10/2005 09/2007	--	--	--	--	09/2007	--	--	--
354305078295801	WC-3S	na	10/2005	10/2005 04/2006	10/2005 04/2006	04/2006	04/2006	04/2006	04/2006	--	--	--	--
354305078295802	WC-3I	na	10/2005	10/2005 04/2006	10/2005 04/2006	04/2006	04/2006	04/2006	04/2006	--	--	--	--
354305078295803	WC-3D	na	10/2005	10/2005	10/2005 09/2007	--	--	--	--	--	--	--	--
354305078295803	WC-3D	41–70	--	03/2006	03/2006	03/2006	03/2006	--	03/2006	--	--	--	--
354305078295803	WC-3D	148–164	--	03/2006	03/2006	03/2006	03/2006	--	03/2006	--	--	--	--
354305078295804	WC-3CH	na	--	--	--	--	--	--	--	--	--	--	--
0208739670	Neuse River tribuary near Auburn, NC	na	10/2005	10/2005	10/2005 09/2007	--	--	--	--	09/2007	--	--	--

movement of ground water to and from the Neuse River. Six tag lines were strung across the Neuse River and marked at 10-ft intervals to delineate six lines of section (A–A' through F–F', fig. 4). A surveyor's rod was used to measure depth to streambed at each 10-ft interval along the tag line prior to temperature and drive-point data collection. This depth profile was used as a measuring reference point for the temperature and drive-point depths.

Temperature

Streambed temperature profiles were completed at 80 locations across the six lines of section spanning the Neuse River. Temperatures were measured using a 4.5-ft thermocouple probe (accurate to 0.2 °C) that was pushed into the streambed of the Neuse River at each 10-ft interval along the transect. Temperature measurements were attempted at 0.5, 2.5, and 4.5 ft below the streambed of the Neuse River at each transect location. Temperatures were recorded and then plotted and contoured to create a vertical cross section across each line of section.

Water Quality

Water samples were collected in the bed of the Neuse River at 47 locations across three of the six temperature lines of section between depths of 0.5 ft and 4.0 ft using a retractable drive-point piezometer. A peristaltic pump was used to extract water samples from drive-point piezometers. Water samples were analyzed in the field for temperature, pH, and SC and at the USGS NWQL in Denver, CO, for total nitrate and ammonia.

Geologic Data

Conventional borehole-geophysical logs collected from each of the bedrock and corehole (D and CH) wells are shown in figures 6–11. Caliper, natural gamma, borehole deviation, and short- and long-normal resistivity logs are used to measure physical properties of the rock. These methods provide preliminary information about borehole construction, condition, and lithology (Keys, 1990). Additionally, high-resolution OTV logs were collected in wells WC-1CH, WC-2D, WC-3D, and WC-2CH and are presented in figures 7, 8, 10, and 11, respectively. The OTV logs were analyzed to identify lithology as well as to determine the physical characteristics and orientation of foliations and fractures.

In November 2005, the study area was investigated with a portable magnetometer. This field reconnaissance confirmed the aerial extent of two north-striking diabase dikes (fig. 12) as encountered during drilling of WC-1D and WC-2CH (core description in appendix 2). These dikes are not mapped on the North Carolina geologic map (North Carolina Geological Survey, 1985).

The USGS Mineral Resources Team in Denver, CO, conducted whole-rock geochemical analyses on nine bedrock core samples collected from the three coreholes (three samples per corehole) during drilling activities at the RHRS. Results of the core analyses are listed in table 4. A geologic description of each sample submitted for analysis has been included for reference, and a complete core description for the corehole at each well cluster is included in the appendixes.

Hydrogeologic Data

Fluid-temperature and fluid-specific conductance borehole geophysical logs were collected from wells WC-1D, WC-1CH, WC-2D, WC-3D, and WC-3CH (figs. 6–8, 10, 11). EM-flowmeter logs were collected under hydraulically stressed and ambient conditions from WC-2D and WC-3D to determine the hydraulic properties of the fractures open to the borehole (figs. 8, 10). The fluid-specific conductance logs can be combined with the temperature and flowmeter logs to identify flow zones and to determine the relative dissolved-solids concentration of the water in the borehole under ambient and stressed conditions (Williams and Conger, 1990).

Periodic water levels were measured in all 12 wells from May 2005 through September 2007 and in the 4 piezometers from February through July 2006 (fig. 13). Ground-water altitudes at well cluster WC-1 ranged from about 146 to 151 ft in the shallow and transition zones and about 140 to 153 ft in the bedrock zone. The shallow and transition zone water levels are affected by the close proximity of the Neuse River. Ground-water altitudes at well cluster WC-2 ranged from about 170 to 174 ft in the shallow and transition zones and about 171 to 180 ft in the bedrock zone. The water-level altitudes in the bedrock zone were consistently higher than water-level altitudes in the shallow and transition zones at well cluster WC-2. Ground-water altitudes at well cluster WC-3 ranged from about 190 to 194 ft. Ground-water altitudes in the piezometers ranged from about 147 to 152 feet. Detailed summaries of ground-water-level data are recorded in the RHRS wells for water years 2005 through 2007 and published in USGS annual data reports for North Carolina (U.S. Geological Survey, 2007).

Continuous ground-water levels were recorded in eight wells, and stage was recorded in the Neuse River (station 0208739677). Ground-water levels were recorded hourly in all the wells in clusters WC-1 and WC-2. The period of data collection for each well varied (table 2). Stage at station 0208739677 Neuse River below SR2555 near Auburn, NC, was recorded in 15-minute intervals from April to June 2006, but the stage recorder was discontinued because it was destroyed by tropical storm Alberto. Continuous gage height at station 0208739677 and continuous water-level altitude at all wells in cluster WC-1 were plotted (fig. 14). For purposes of comparison, stage at station 02087500 Neuse River near Clayton (approximately 10 miles downstream from the RHRS)

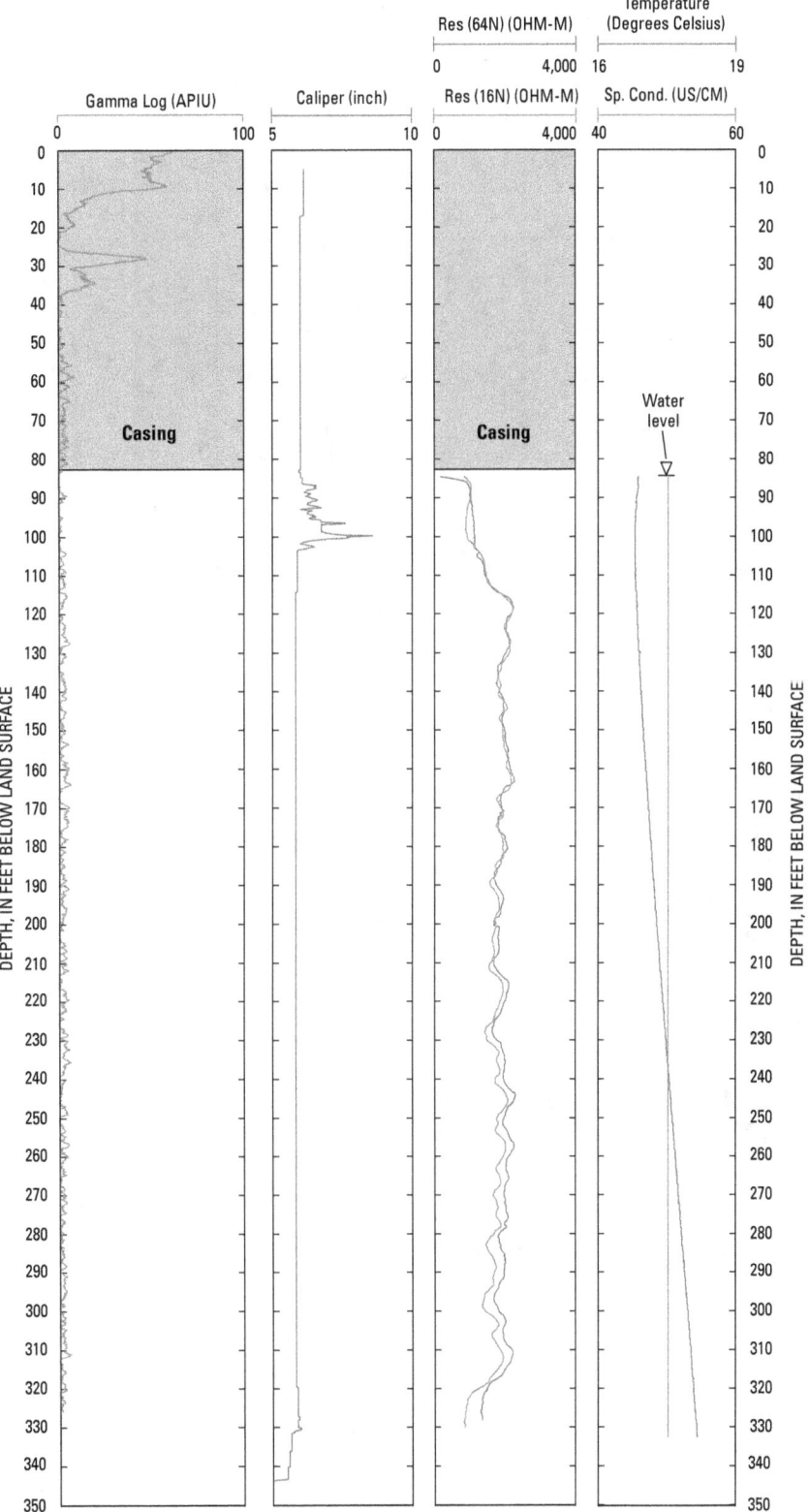

Figure 6   Geophysical logs for bedrock well WC-1D at the Raleigh hydrogeologic research station, North Carolina.

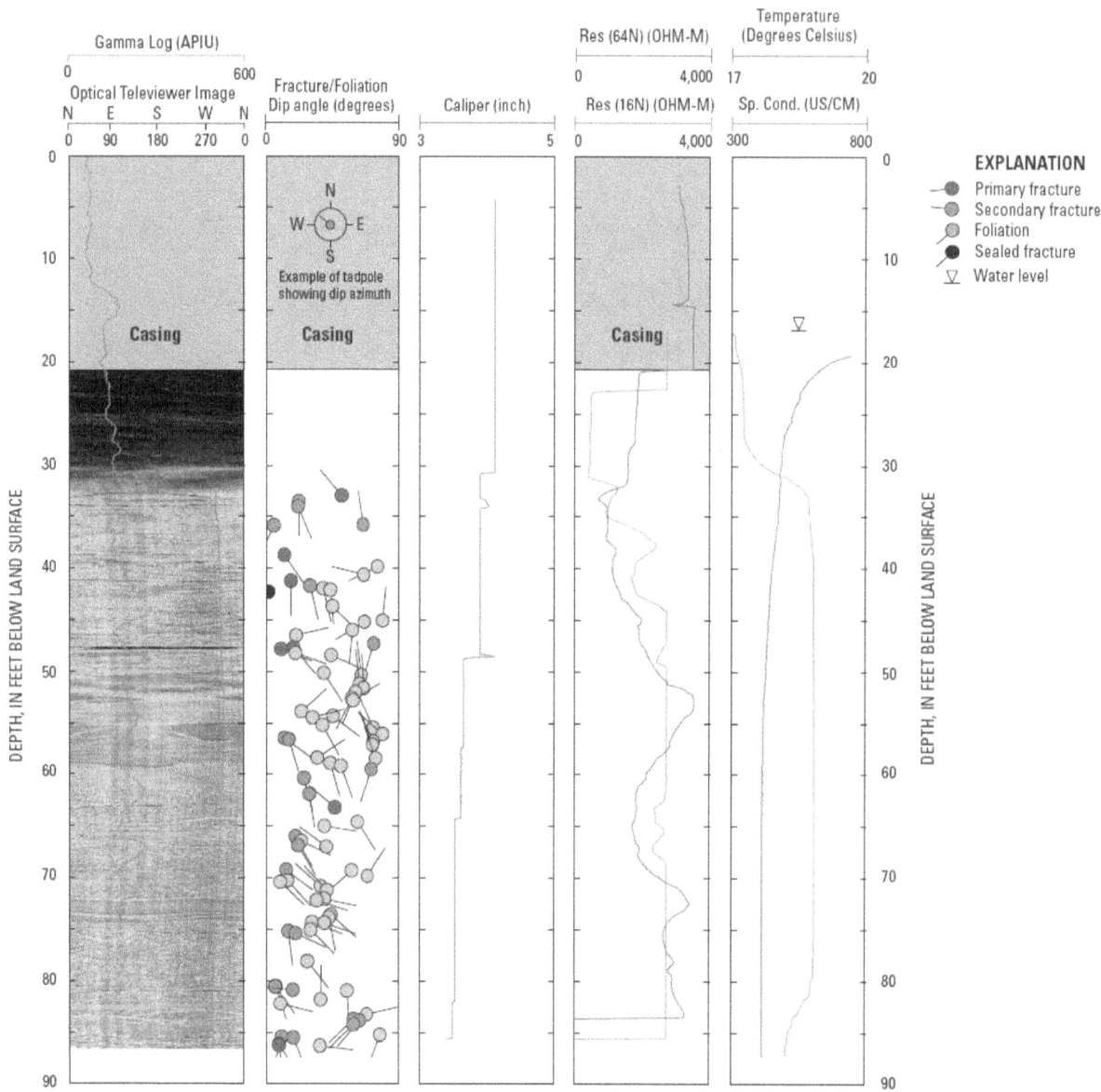

Figure 7   Geophysical logs for bedrock well WC-1CH at the Raleigh hydrogeologic research station, North Carolina.

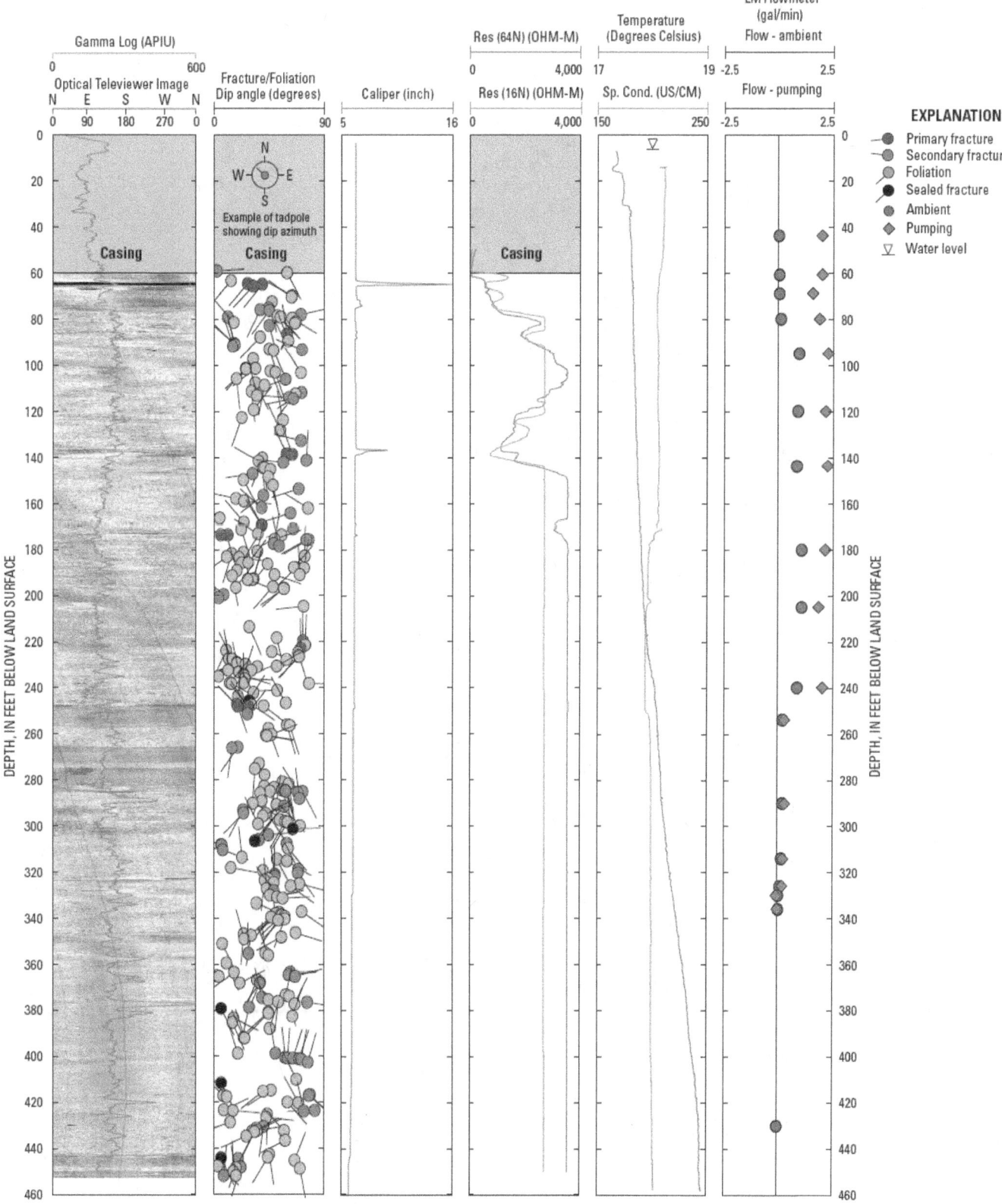

Figure 8   Geophysical logs for bedrock well WC-2D at the Raleigh hydrogeologic research station, North Carolina.

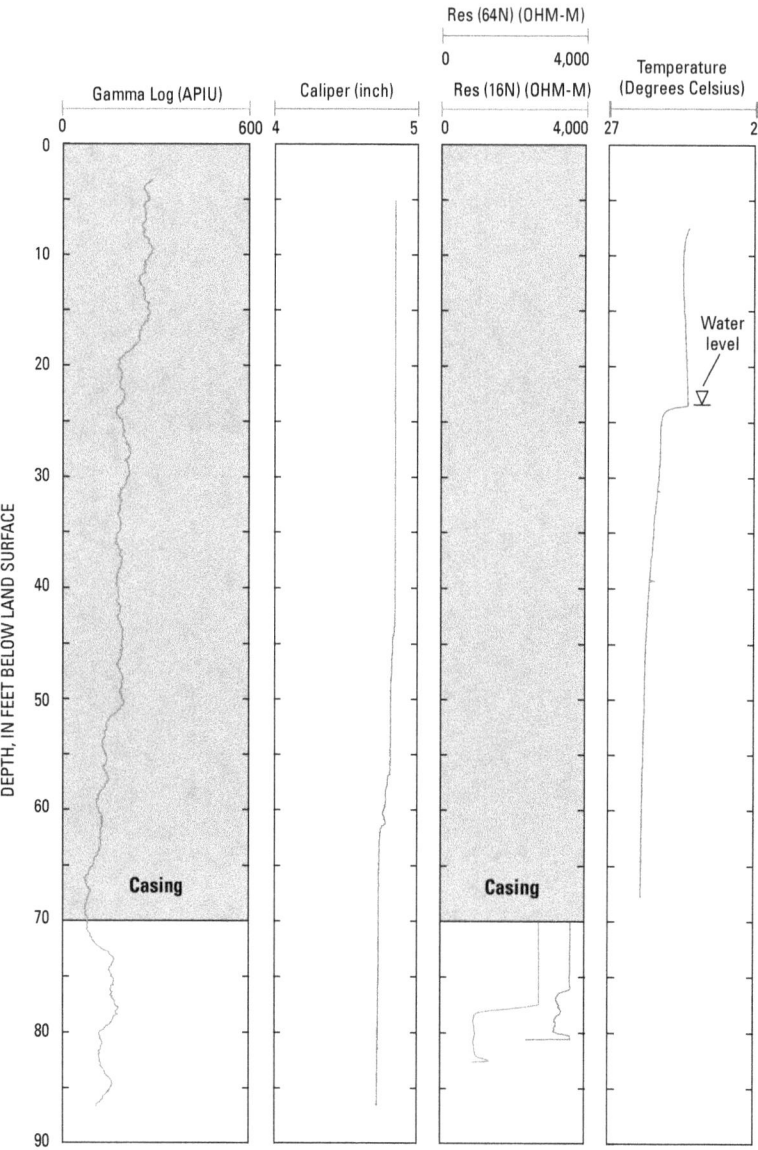

Figure 9.   Geophysical logs for bedrock well WC-2CH at the Raleigh hydrogeologic research station, North Carolina.

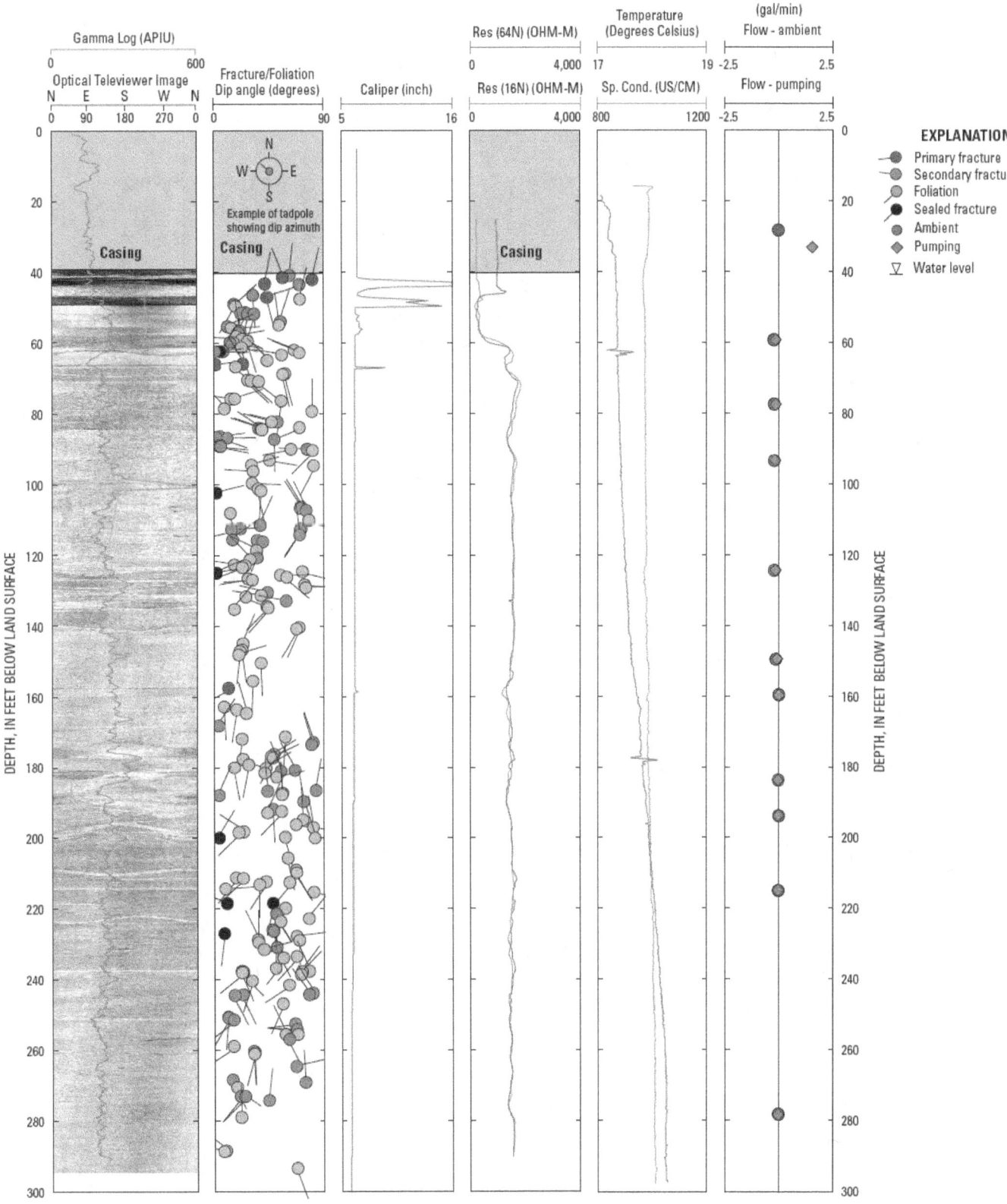

Figure 10   Geophysical logs for bedrock well WC-3D at the Raleigh hydrogeologic research station, North Carolina.

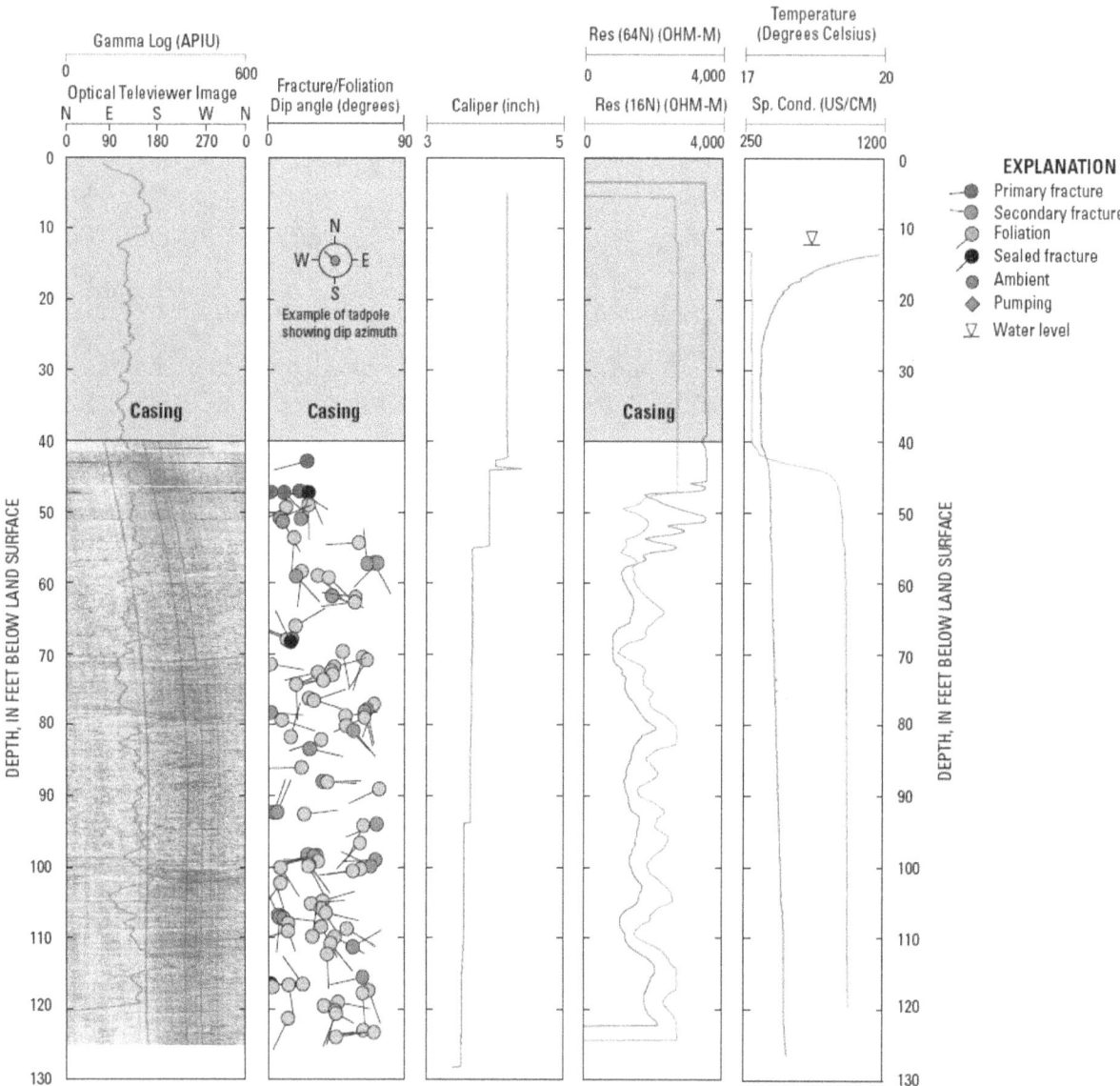

Figure 11.   Geophysical logs for bedrock well WC-3CH at the Raleigh hydrogeologic research station, North Carolina.

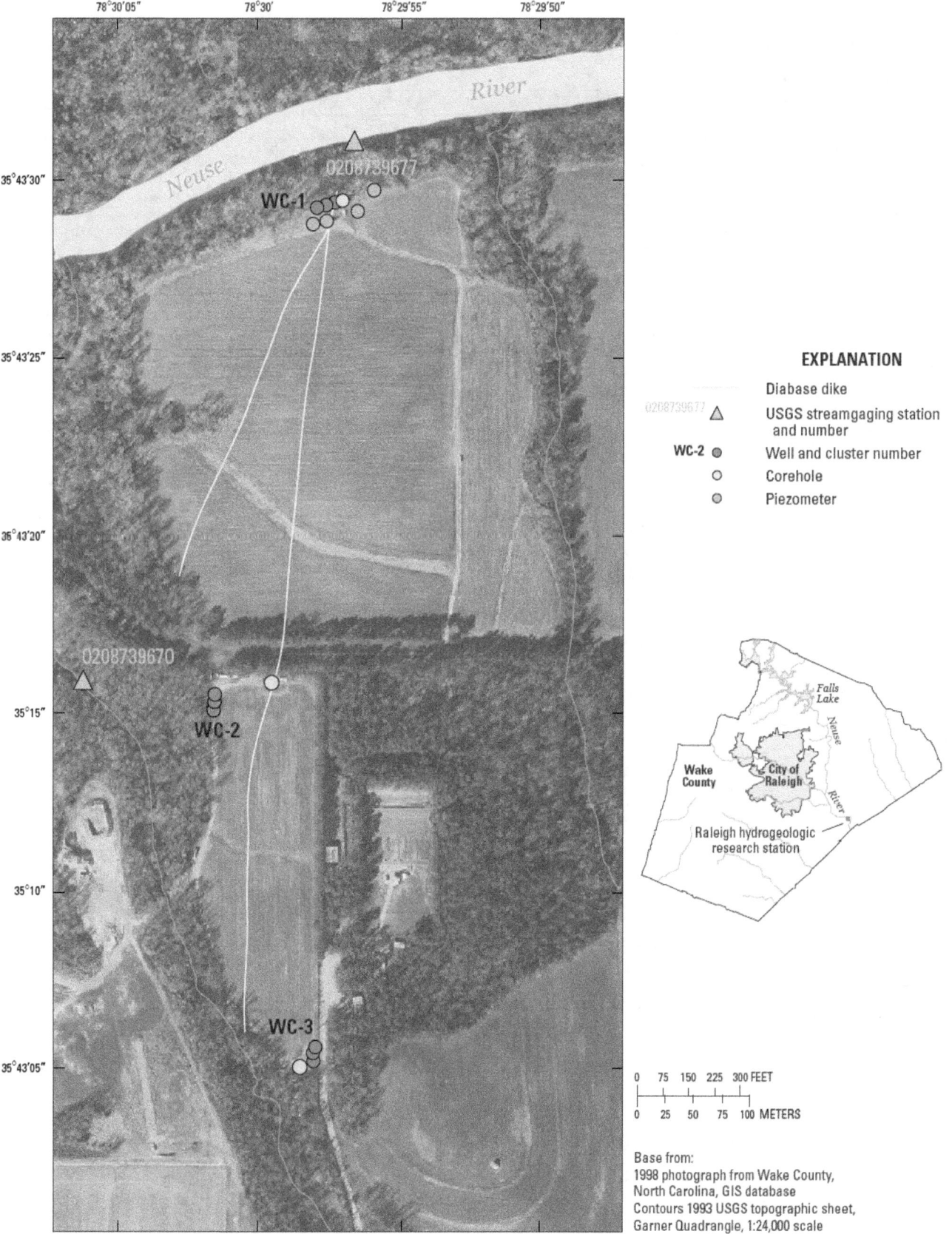

Figure 12.   Aerial photograph of the Raleigh hydrogeologic research station, Wake County, North Carolina, overlaid with approximate projected surface location of diabase dikes from magnetometer data.

Table 4. Analytical results of average whole-rock core samples and geologic description of the whole-rock core samples collected during drilling activities at the Raleigh hydrogeologic research station, Wake County, North Carolina.

[ft bls, feet below land surface; ppm, part per million; %, percent]

Element	Reporting unit	WC-1CH			WC-2CH			WC-3CH		
		Sampled depth (ft bls)								
		41.4	59.6	70.0	57.7	78.9	103.5	48.5	66.3	117.3
Iron	%	1.48	1.62	1.94	8.42	10.00	1.54	1.44	1.15	1.18
Calcium	%	0.93	1.53	1.52	0.44	6.81	0.99	1.23	1.05	0.82
Sodium	%	3.11	3.02	3.19	0.90	1.87	3.45	2.98	2.67	2.75
Potassium	%	3.28	3.06	2.65	2.35	0.26	2.76	2.87	3.45	3.07
Rhubidium	ppm	127	125	137	105	10.35	133	173	148	163
Strontium	ppm	384	490	374	180	181	360	364	319	252
Cesium	ppm	2.38	2.57	4.12	4.88	0.76	2.02	7.47	3.78	2.96
Barium	ppm	787	1195	907	709	60	1180	1050	855	674
Thorium	ppm	15.8	13.4	18.4	13.0	0.15	17.2	22.7	17.5	15.4
Uranium	ppm	3.54	2.09	3.92	23.0	0.17	1.79	4.53	2.63	2.81
Lanthanum	ppm	34.6	36.2	42.8	24.7	2.44	46.1	23.2	25.4	20.6
Cerium	ppm	60.1	66.8	77.6	43.6	5.98	77.1	65.6	48.5	40.9
Neodymium	ppm	20.7	24.5	28.4	17.3	4.17	28.5	17.3	18.5	15.2
Samarium	ppm	3.10	4.02	4.84	3.78	1.53	4.21	3.12	3.11	2.85
Europium	ppm	0.68	0.87	0.89	0.87	0.66	0.97	0.70	0.69	0.65
Gadolinium	ppm	2.62	3.11	3.72	3.83	2.38	3.02	2.75	2.57	2.54
Terbium	ppm	0.24	0.30	0.45	0.55	0.55	0.26	0.29	0.24	0.31
Holmium	ppm	0.26	0.31	0.49	0.76	0.94	0.23	0.35	0.23	0.32
Thulium	ppm	0.08	0.10	0.15	0.32	0.45	0.06	0.14	0.08	0.11
Ytterbium	ppm	0.51	0.56	0.89	1.96	2.82	0.38	0.83	0.46	0.62
Lutetium	ppm	0.08	0.08	0.13	0.30	0.44	0.06	0.13	0.07	0.09
Zirconium	ppm	166	195	254	122[a]	38.7	268	173	150	145
Hafnium	ppm	4.46	4.75	6.28	3.38	1.05	6.25	4.57	4.07	4.06
Tantalum	ppm	0.50	0.57	1.13	0.99	0.11	0.28	0.94	0.50	0.64
Tungsten	ppm	0.44[b]	0.22[b]	0.18[b]	0.07[b]	0.54	0.28[a,b]	0.38[c]	0.29	0.35
Scandium	ppm	3.46	3.61	4.33	14.4	34.1	2.34	3.65	2.75	3.31
Chromium	ppm	8.55	12.60	9.94	161	455	4.60	6.75	6.75	7.59
Cobalt	ppm	3.30	4.87	4.91	41.3	70.7	4.42	3.64	2.67	2.50
Nickel	ppm	4.24	7.57	7.19	75.50	277	5.59	3.69	4.63	4.97
Zinc	ppm	47.8	54.2	72.0	64.3	70.9	56.6	49.7	40.9	43.6
Arsenic	ppm	0.17	0.07	0.09	0.72	0.13	0.15	0.10	0.17	0.23
Antimony	ppm	0.04	0.02	0.04	0.05	0.02	0.01	0.06	0.07	0.04
Gold	ppb	1.14[a]	0.66[a]	0.64[a]	0.72[a]	3.69	0.59[a]	1.24[a]	0.61[a]	0.35[a]

[a]Coefficient of variation exceeds 30 percent.

[b]Interference correction exceeds 60 percent.

[c]Below empirical detection limit.

Corehole sample	Geologic description
WC-1CH 40.0 ft bls	Micaceous, coarse-grained, lightly weathered granitoid with iron oxide on surfaces
WC-1CH 59.6 ft bls	Very fine-grained micaceous granitoid with pure feldspathic vein
WC-1CH 70.0 ft bls	Weathered fine-grained micaceous granitoid (typical of core)
WC-2CH 57.7 ft bls	Highly weathered, vertically fractured granitoid, possibly "pegmatite", typical Rolesville Granite
WC-2CH 78.9 ft bls	Mafic (diabase), fine-grained, unfractured
WC-2CH 103.5 ft bls	Typical Rolesville Granite, fine grained, with surface coatings of iron
WC-3CH 48.5 ft bls	Solid, fine-grained biotite-muscovite granitoid, unfractured, unweathered, minor iron coatings
WC-3CH 66.3 ft bls	Coarse to pegmatitic granitoid
WC-3CH 117.3 ft bls	Fine-grained gray granitoid

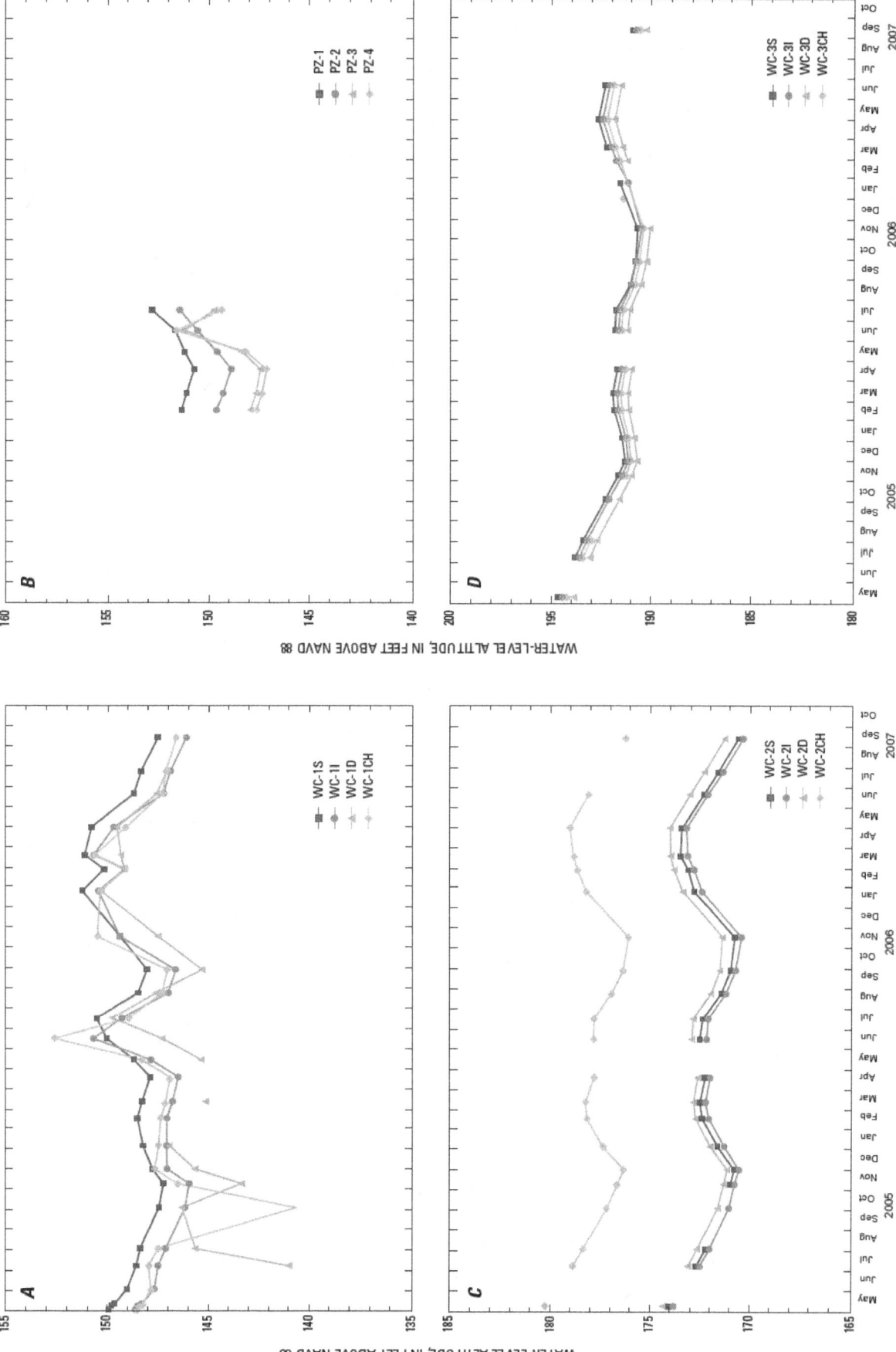

Figure 13   Periodic ground-water levels recorded in well cluster WC-1, piezometers at WC-1, well cluster WC-2, and well cluster WC-3 at the Raleigh hydrogeologic research station, North Carolina, from May 2005 to September 2007.

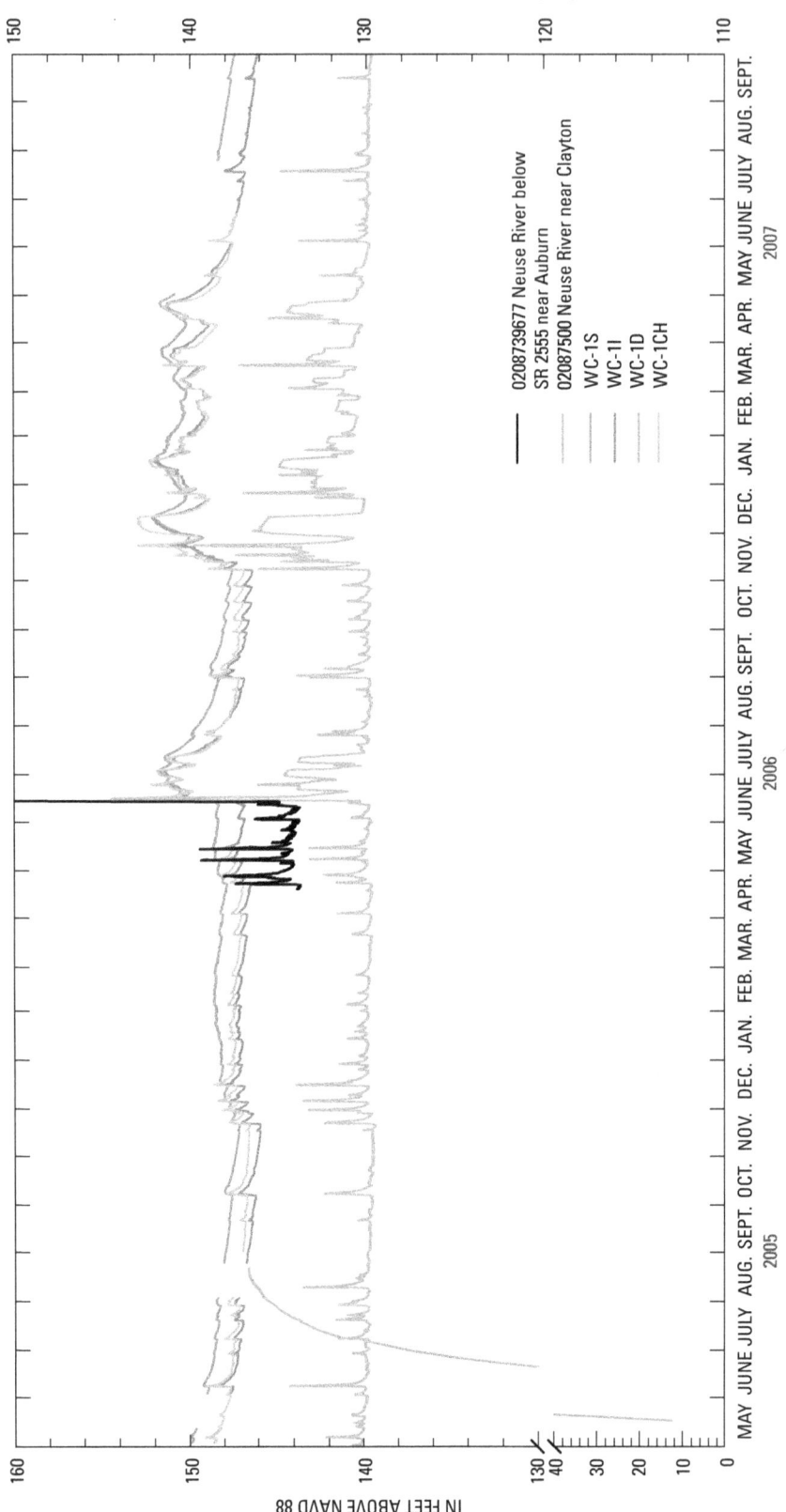

Figure 14. Hourly ground-water levels recorded in well cluster WC-1 and hourly stage recorded at surface-water stations 0208739677 and 02087500 at the Raleigh hydrogeologic research station, North Carolina, from May 2005 to September 2007.

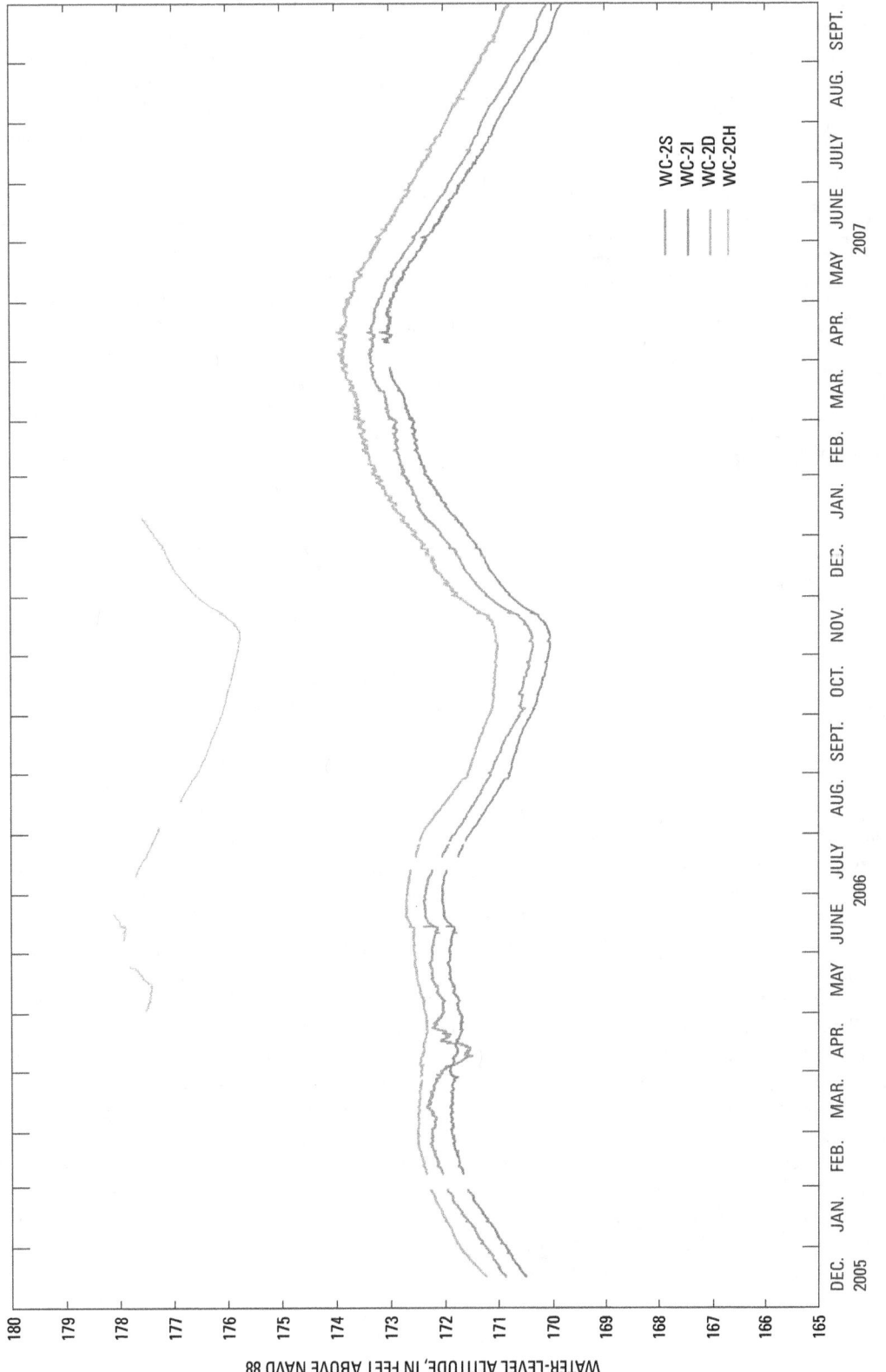

Figure 15. Hourly ground-water levels recorded in well cluster WC-2 at the Raleigh hydrogeologic research station, North Carolina, from December 2005 to September 2007.

was plotted in figure 14 as it correlates well with the limited stage data collected at station 0208739677. Continuous water-level altitude in cluster WC-2 was plotted in figure 15.

Slug tests were conducted at the RHRS in March and July 2007. The slug tests were conducted to obtain estimates

Table 5. Analytical results of slug tests in wells at the Raleigh hydrogeologic research station, North Carolina.

Well number	Screened/open interval (feet below land surface)	Hydraulic conductivity (feet per day)
Regolith wells		
WC-1S	13–28	0.8
WC-2S	13.5–28.5	7
WC-3S	13.6–28.5	6
Transition-zone wells		
WC-1I	24–39	2
WC-2I	27–42	5
WC-3I	34–49	5
Bedrock wells		
WC-1CH	21–90	0.6
WC-2D	59–440	10
WC-2CH	70–85	3
WC-3D	40–300	4
WC-3CH	40–125	0.4

of hydraulic conductivity in the aquifer zones tapped by the wells. The estimates obtained are representative of conditions in the immediate vicinity of the tested wells. The wells and intervals tested and the hydraulic conductivity values are listed in table 5.

Water-quality samples were collected from an unnamed Neuse River tributary (station 0208739670, fig. 4) near well cluster WC-2 and all wells (excluding the piezometers) at the RHRS twice, once in October 2005 and again in April 2006. During the second sampling event (April 2006), the multifunction BAT[3] (Shapiro, 2001) inflatable packer system was used in the bedrock wells to isolate fracture zones. Water-quality-data results are displayed in Piper diagrams for all sampling dates (fig. 16) and in Stiff diagrams for October 2005 (fig. 17). Major ion water chemistry in periodic samples from the regolith, transition zone, and the tributary samples is shown in Piper plots in figure 16A; major ion water chemistry

in periodic samples from the open borehole bedrock wells at the RHRS is shown in Piper plots in figure 16B. Ranges of water-quality-data results for all sampling dates are displayed in box plots in figures 18–20.

Continuous water-quality data were collected from December 2005 through January 2007 in three wells in cluster WC-2 and from May to June 2006 in the unnamed Neuse River tributary (station 0208739670). Hourly temperature, pH, SC, and DO concentrations were collected in wells WC-2S (regolith), WC-2I (transition zone), and WC-2D (bedrock; figs. 21–23; table 2). Temperature, pH, and SC were collected every 15 minutes at station 0208739670 (fig. 24; table 2). Temperature at well cluster WC-2 ranged from about 15.9 to 17.2 °C in the regolith well, from about 16.0 to 16.7 °C in the transition zone, and from about 16.0 to 16.2 °C in the bedrock. Specific conductance ranged from about 800 to 1,150 micro-siemens per centimeter (µS/cm) at 25 °C in the regolith, from about 570 to 1,150 µS/cm in the transition zone, and from about 260 to 330 µS/cm in the bedrock. Dissolved-oxygen concentrations ranged from about 6.4 to 7.6 milligrams per liter (mg/L) in the regolith, 4.3 to 5.9 mg/L in the transition zone, and 0.2 to 1.5 mg/L in the bedrock. Recorded values of pH ranged from about 4.3 to 5.1 in the regolith, from about 4.8 to 5.3 in the transition zone, and from about 7.4 to 7.7 in the bedrock. Water temperature in the unnamed Neuse River tributary ranged from about 12.0 to 20.0 °C, SC ranged from about 190 to 650 µS/cm, and pH ranged from about 6.6 to 7.3.

Waterborne continuous resistivity profiling was conducted on the Neuse River in the area of the NRWWTP to measure the apparent resistivity distribution of the sediments, weathered rock, and pore-water fluid beneath the streambed. Composition of the sediment and weathered rock, amount of water in the pore space and fractures, ionic concentration of the pore fluid, and variations in pore space affect resistivity. An example of a processed inversion of one continuous resistivity profile section of the Neuse River near the study area is presented in figure 25.

Streambed temperatures were measured and ground-water samples were collected across the Neuse River at three of the lines of section during a 3-day period in August 2006. Locations of the lines of sections are shown in figure 4. Measured temperatures ranged from about 15 °C to 30 °C. Water-quality samples were analyzed for total nitrate and ammonia concentration. Nitrate concentrations ranged from undetected (<0.060 mg/L) to about 80 mg/L, and ammonia concentrations ranged from undetected (<0.010 mg/L) to about 6.6 mg/L. Cross sections displaying contoured temperature measurements, the locations of ground-water samples, and the concentrations of nitrate and ammonia are shown in figures 26, 27, and 28.

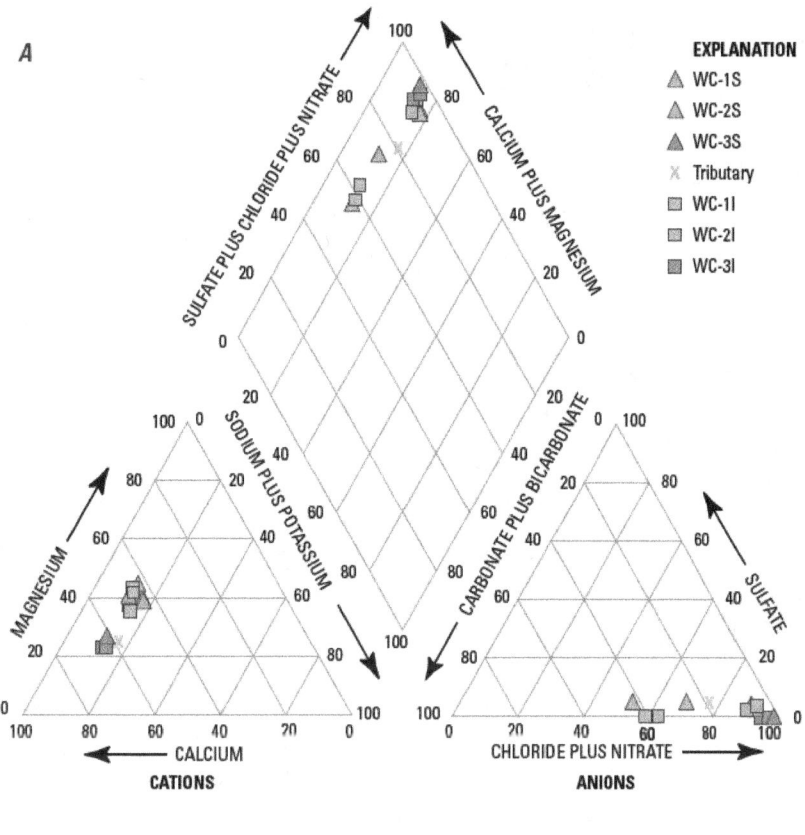

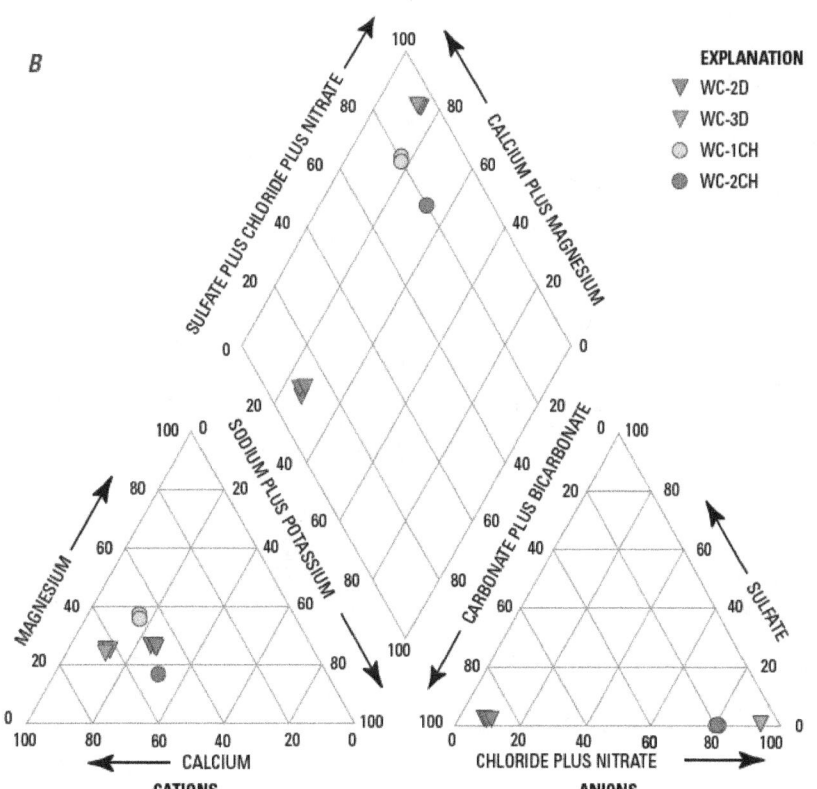

Figure 16.   The water chemistry of samples from regolith and transition-zone wells and the tributary site, and bedrock wells at the Raleigh hydrogeologic research station, North Carolina.

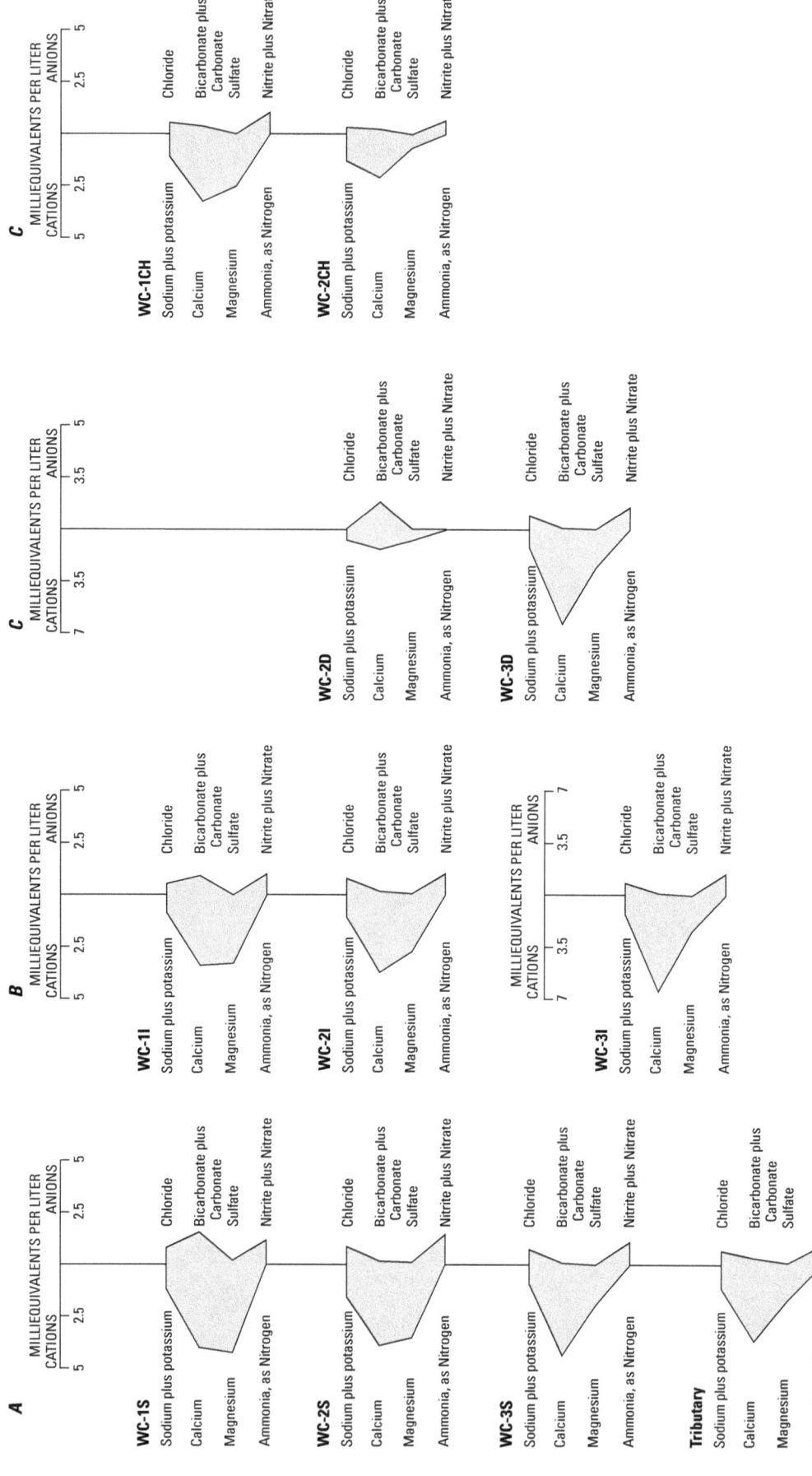

Figure 17. Major ion milliequivalents in water samples collected from regolith wells and the Neuse River tributary site (0208739670), transition-zone wells, and open-borehole bedrock wells at the Raleigh hydrogeologic research station, North Carolina, October 2005.

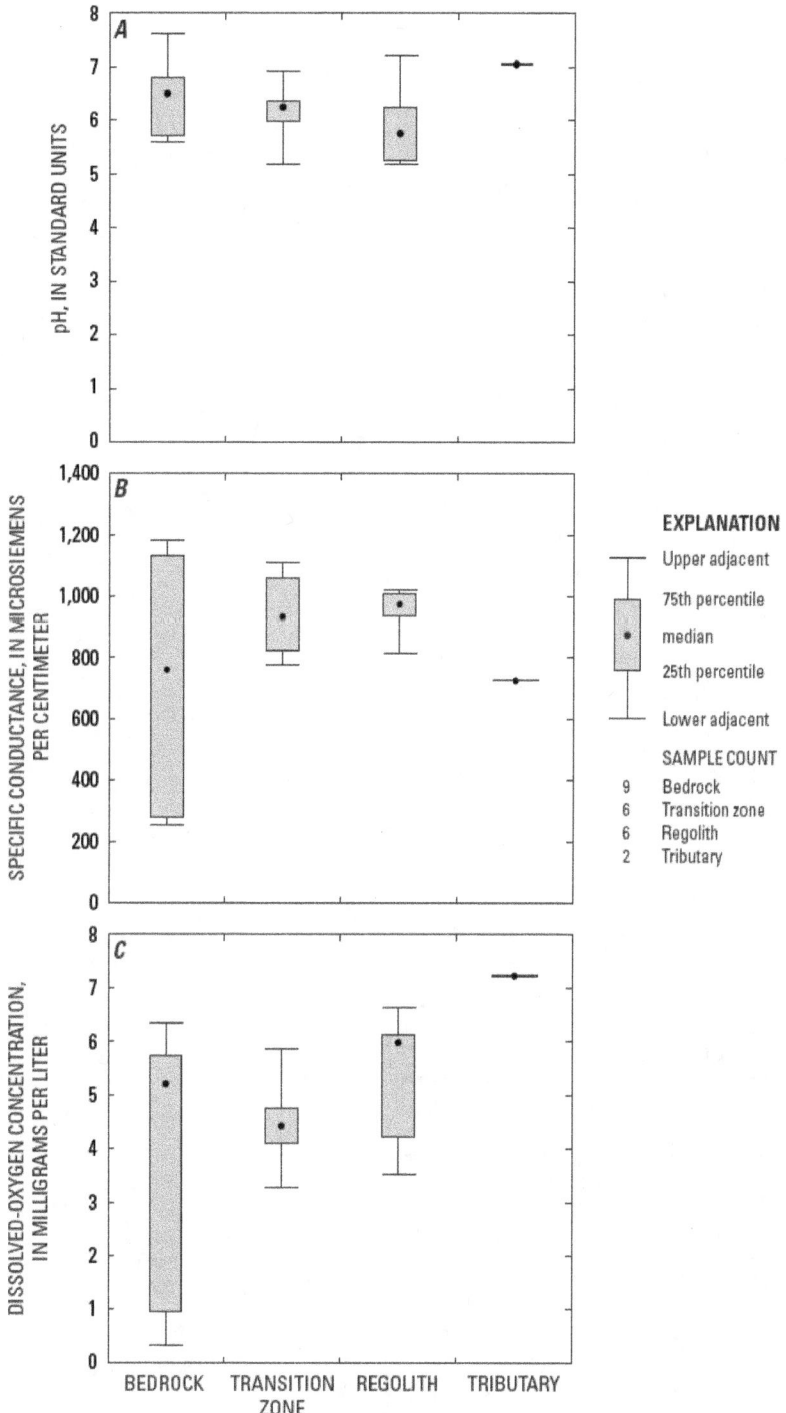

Figure 18. Box plots showing range, median, and quartile statistica values for pH, specific conductance, and dissolved-oxygen concentration in the wells and tributary recorded du ing periodic sampling events at the Raleigh hydrogeo ogic research station.

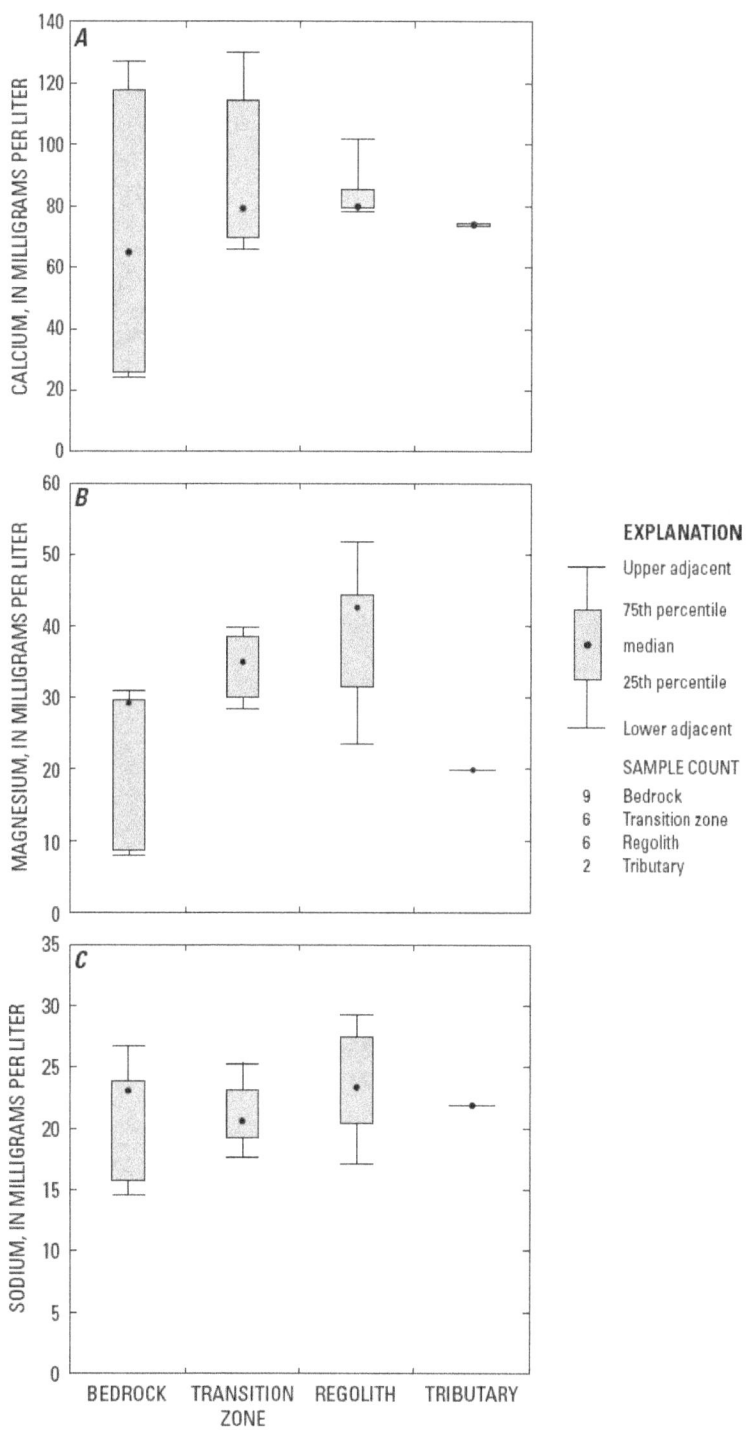

Figure 19. Box plots showing range, median, and quart le statistical values for ca cium, magnesium, and sodi m in the wells and tributary recorded during periodic sampling events at the Raleigh hydrogeologic resea ch station.

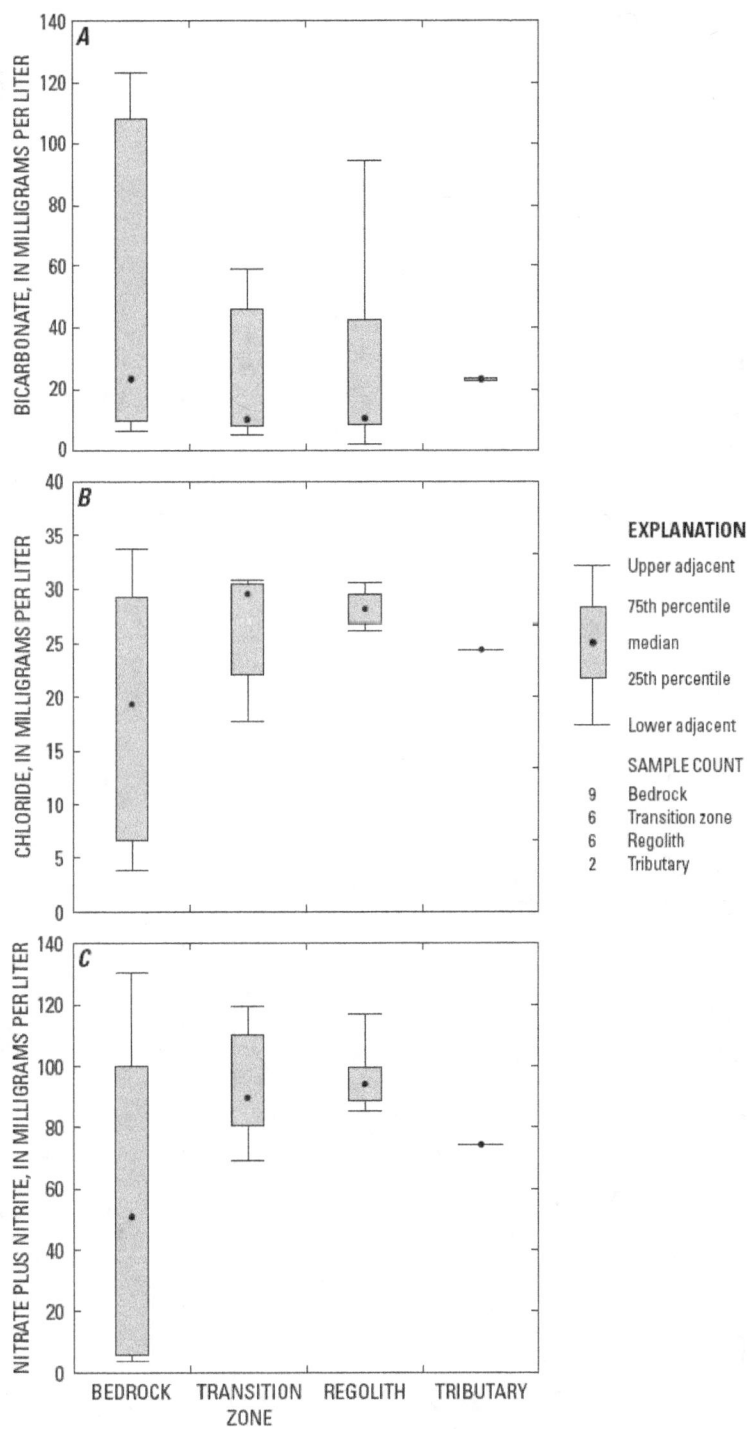

Figure 20.   Box plots showing range median, and quart le statistical values for bicarbonate, chloride and nitrate plus nitrite in the wells and tributary recorded during periodic sampling events at the Raleigh hydrogeologic research station.

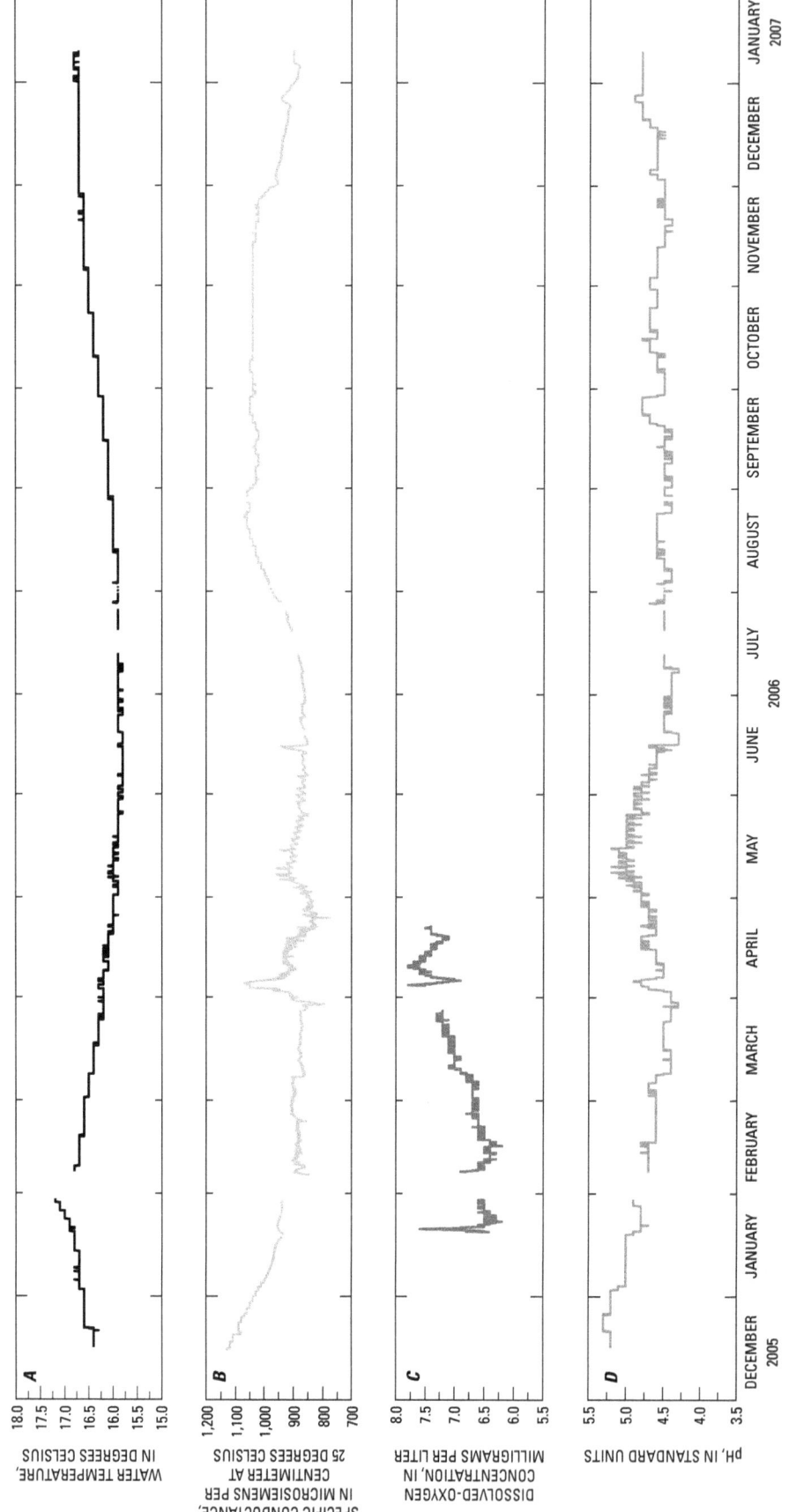

Figure 21. Hourly record of temperature, specific conductance, dissolved-oxygen concentration, and pH in well WC-2S in the shallow regolith at the Raleigh hydrogeologic research station, North Carolina, December 2005 through January 2007.

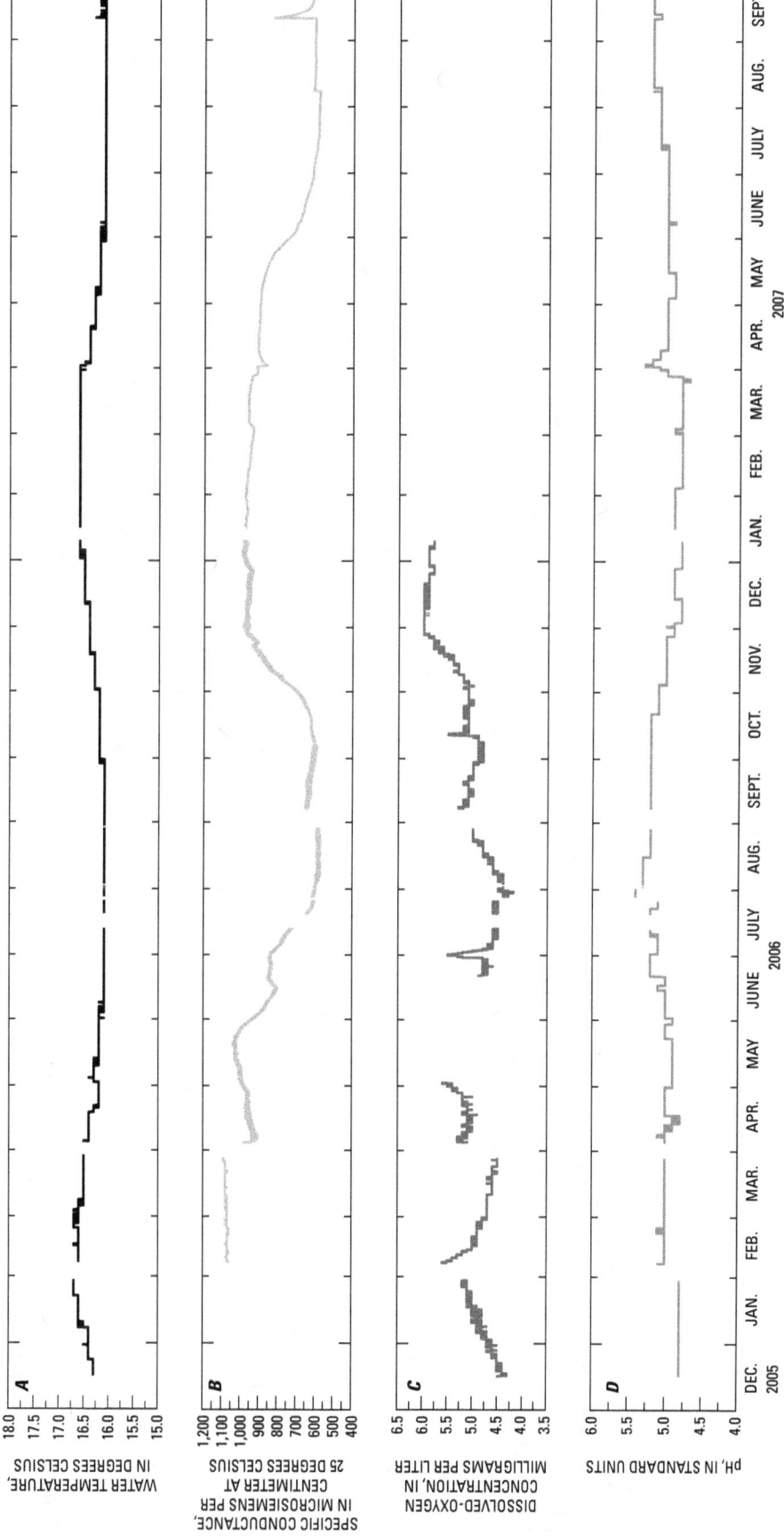

Figure 22. Hourly record of temperature, specific conductance, dissolved-oxygen concentration, and pH in well WC-2I in the transition zone at the Raleigh hydrogeologic research station, North Carolina, December 2005 through September 2007.

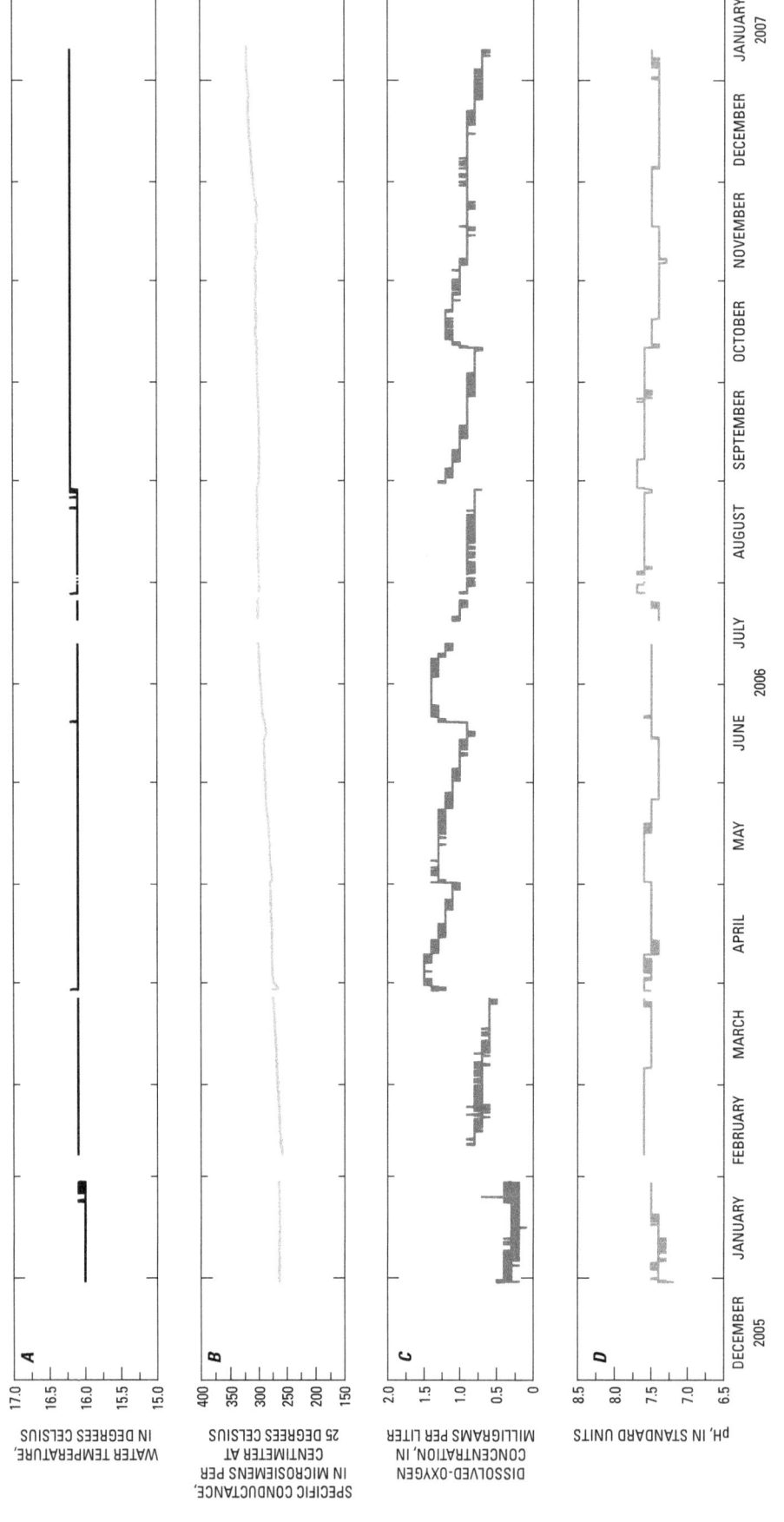

Figure 23. Hourly record of (A) temperature, (B) specific conductance, (C) dissolved-oxygen concentration, and (D) pH in well WC-2D in the bedrock at the Raleigh hydrogeologic research station, North Carolina, December 2005 through January 2007.

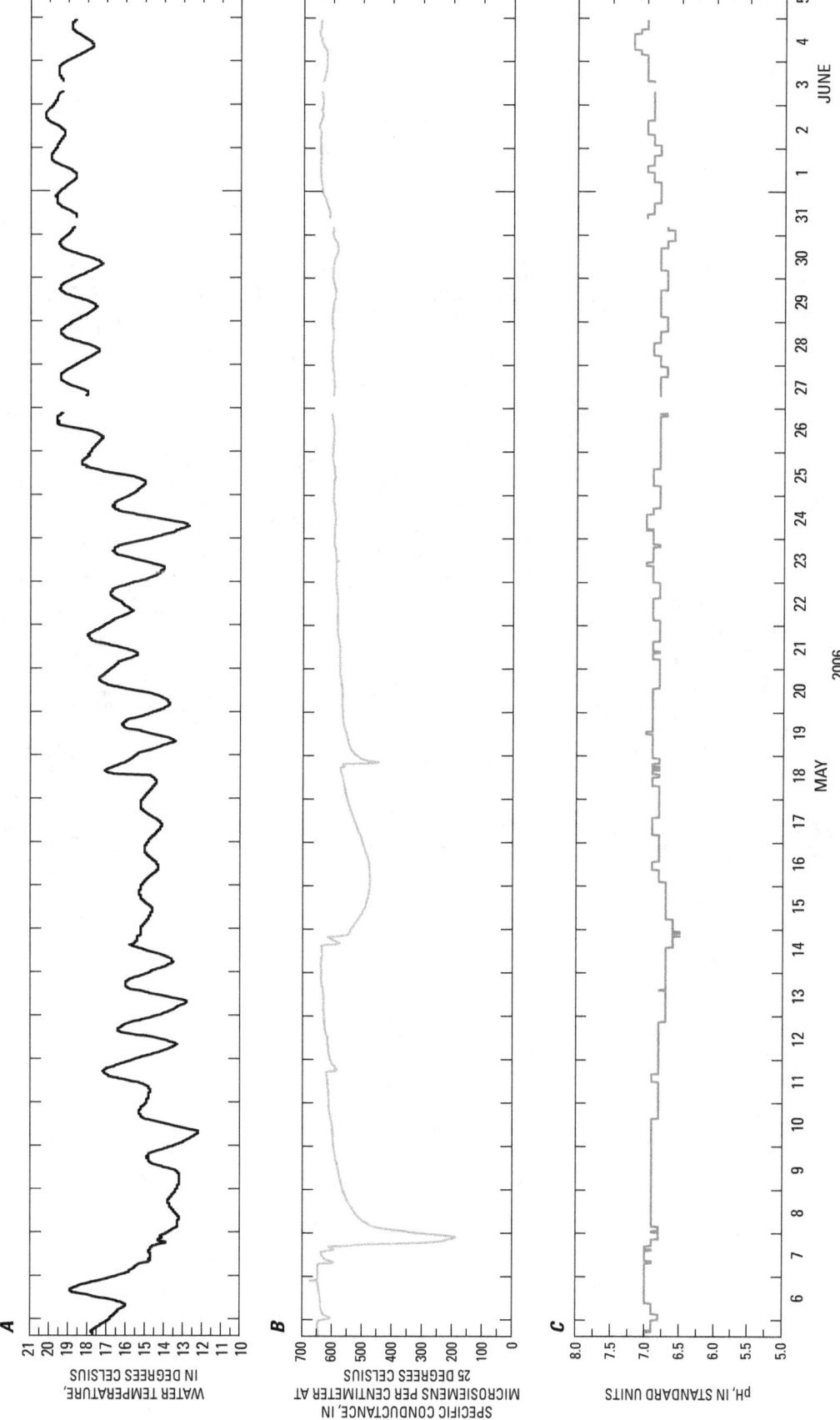

Figure 24   Fifteen-minute record of (A) temperature, (B) specific conductance, and (C) pH at station 0208739670 Neuse River tributary near Auburn, North Carolina, May through June 2006.

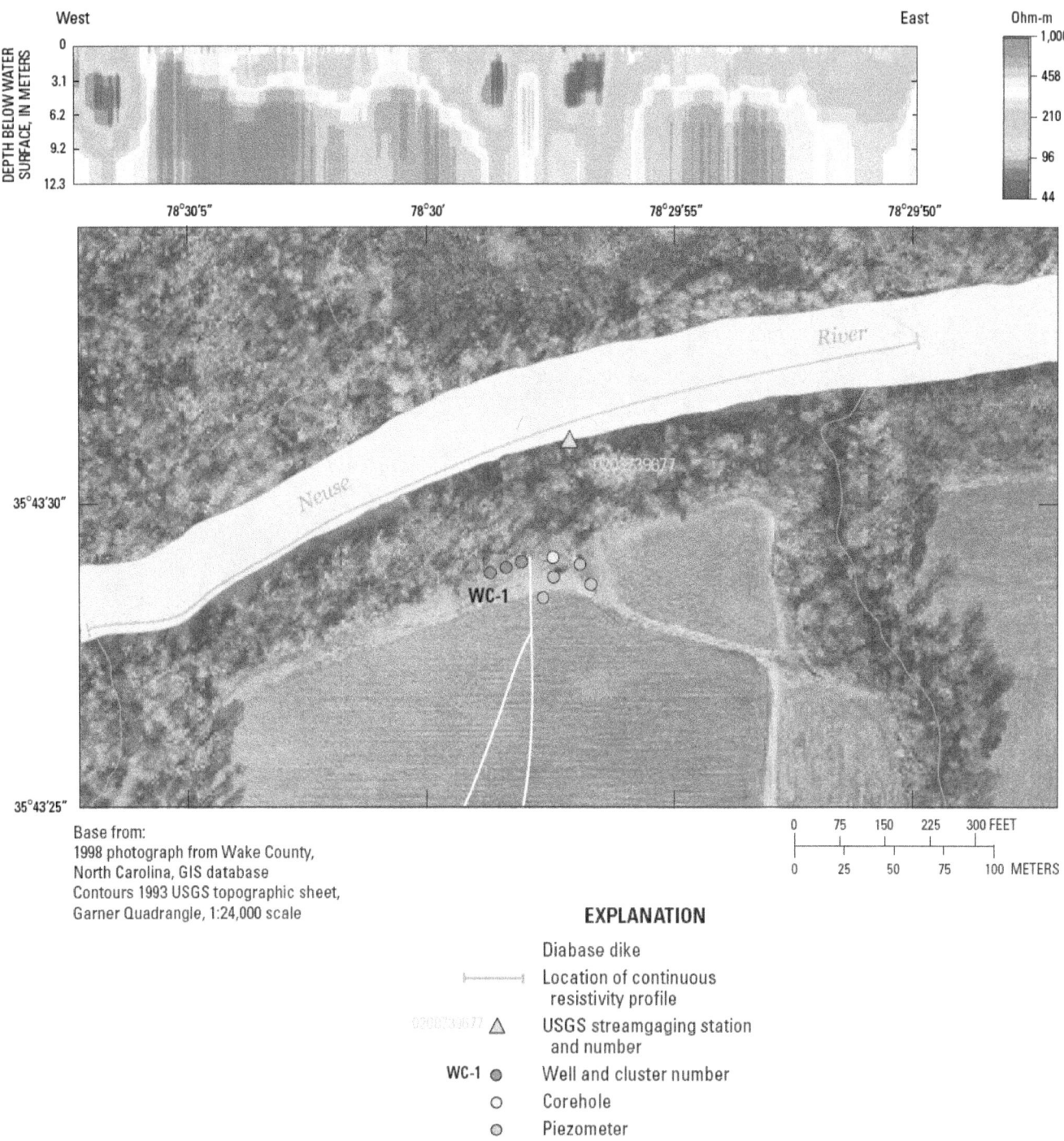

Figure 25.   Processed continuous resistivity profile (CRP) inversion and location of CRP survey with approximate projected surface location of diabase dikes from magnetometer data overlaid on an aerial photograph of the Raleigh hydrogeologic research station, Wake County, North Carolina.

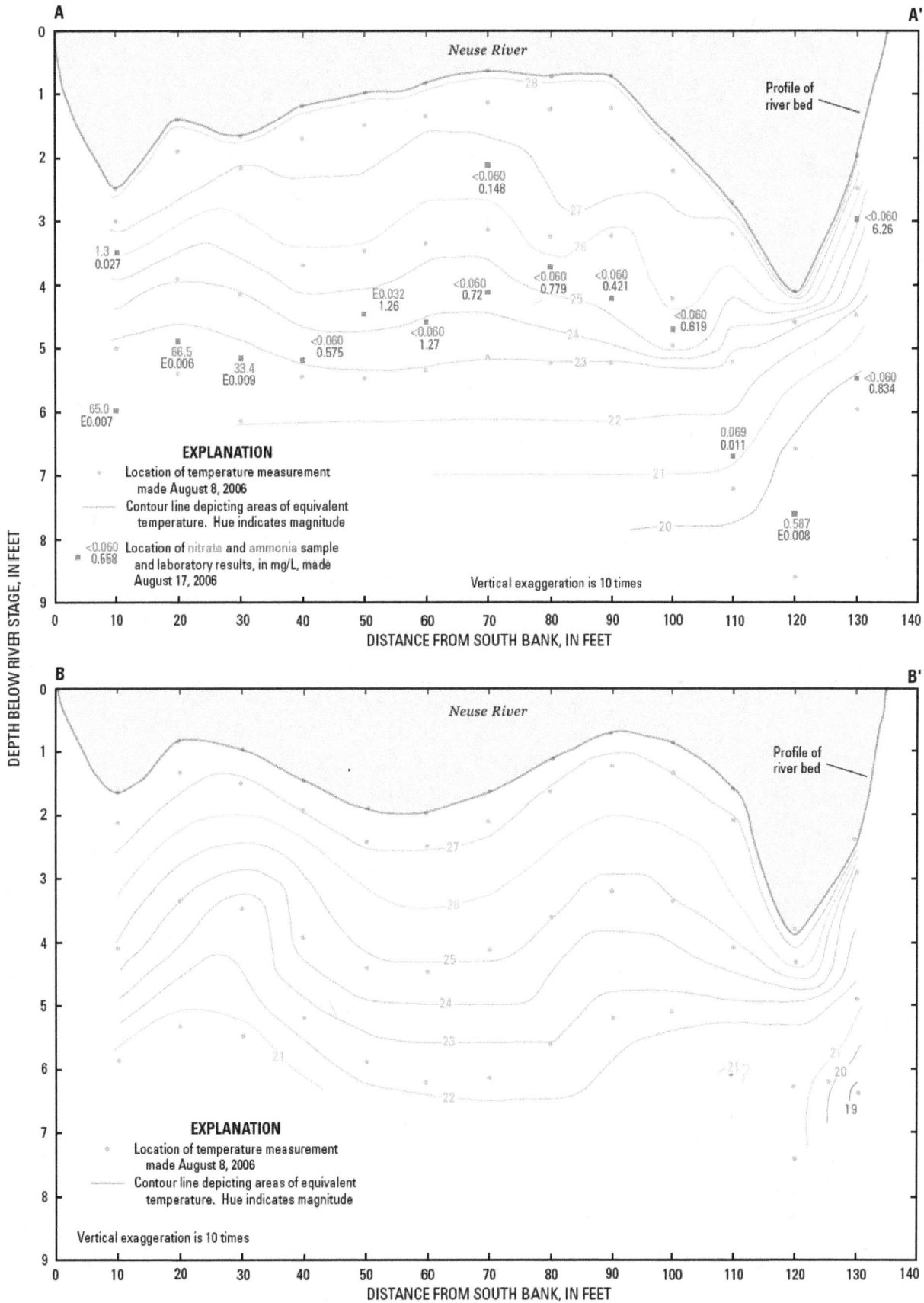

Figure 26. Ground-water temperature and concentration of total nitrate and ammonia beneath the Neuse River at lines of section A–A′ and B–B′.

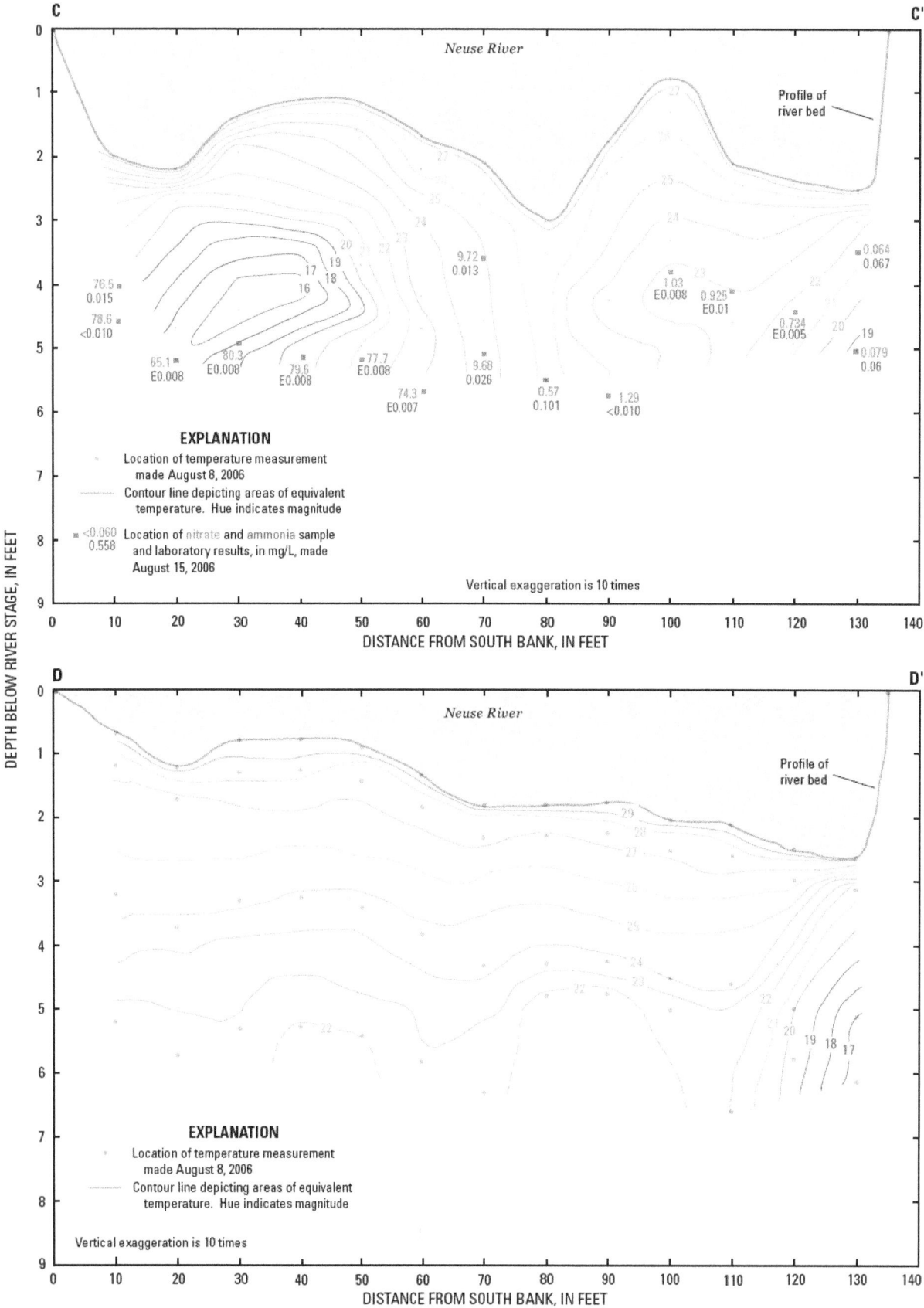

Figure 27.   Ground-water temperature and concentration of total nitrate and ammonia beneath the Neuse River at lines of section C–C′ and D–D′.

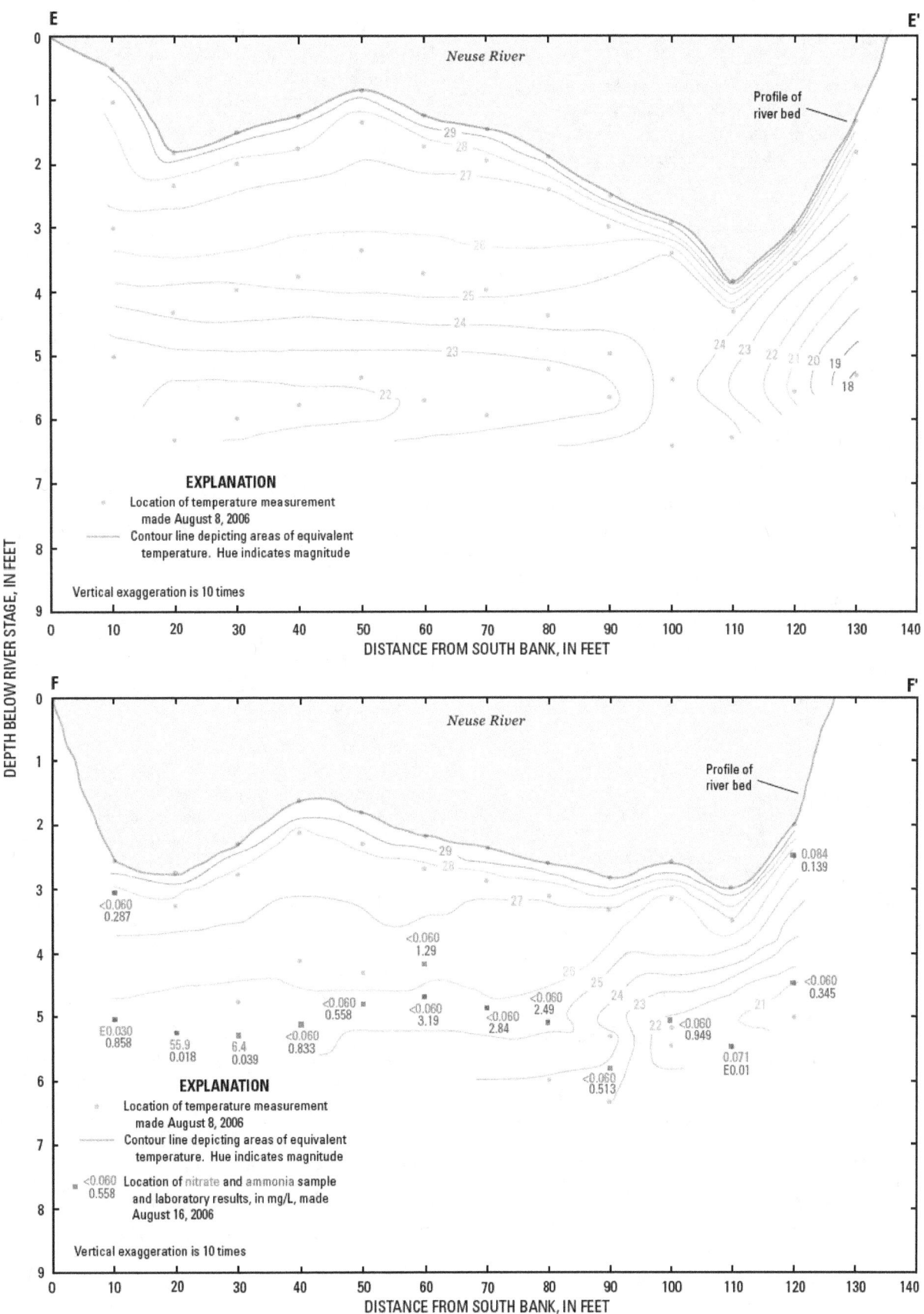

Figure 28. Ground-water temperature and concentration of total nitrate and ammonia beneath the Neuse River at lines of section E–E′ and F–F′

Summary

During 2005–07, the U.S. Geological Survey and the North Carolina Department of Environment and Natural Resources, Division of Water Quality, conducted a study to measure ground-water quality and to characterize the ground-water-flow system at the Raleigh hydrogeologic research station in eastern Wake County, North Carolina. Data were collected from 12 wells and 4 piezometers at 3 well clusters and from 80 discrete locations in the streambed of the Neuse River. Data presented in this report include regional surficial geology, research-station design, well characteristics, borehole and surface geophysical data, water-quality data, and water-level data collected at the Raleigh hydrogeologic research station from 2005 through 2007.

Acknowledgments

The authors thank members of the North Carolina Department of Environment and Natural Resources and the USGS Resource Evaluation Program who contributed to data collection for this report. In addition, the authors thank the DWQ drillers for their support of data collection in the field; Tim Woody, Superintendent of the NRWWTP, for his support and assistance in facilitating field-site access; David Vinson of Duke University for his assistance with whole-rock analyses; and Alton Anderson and Eric White of the USGS Office of Ground Water, Branch of Geophysics, for their assistance in collecting geophysical data.

References Cited

Bouwer, H., and Rice, R.C., 1976, A slug test for determining hydraulic conductivity of unconfined aquifers with completely or partially penetrating wells: Water Resources Research, v. 12, no. 3, p. 423–428.

Busenberg, Eurybiades, and Plummer, L.N., 1992, Use of chlorofluoromethanes (CCl3F and CCl2F2) as hydrologic tracers and age-dating tools, Example—the alluvium and terrace system of central Oklahoma: Water Resources Research, v. 28, p. 2257–2283.

Butler, J.J., Jr., 1998, The design, performance, and analysis of slug tests: Boca Raton, FL, Lewis Publishers, 251 p.

Camp Dresser and McKee, Inc., 2003, Wake County comprehensive goundwater investigation: Camp Dresser and McKee, Inc., 147 p.

Chapman, M.J., Bolich, R.E., and Huffman, B.A., 2005, Hydrogeologic setting, ground-water flow, and ground-water quality at the Lake Wheeler Road research station, 2001–03, North Carolina Piedmont and Mountains Resource Evaluation Program: U.S. Geological Survey Scientific Investigations Report 2005–5166, 85 p.

Daniel, C.C., III, and Dahlen, P.R., 2002, Preliminary hydrogeologic assessment and study plan for a regional ground-water resource investigation of the Blue Ridge and Piedmont Provinces of North Carolina: U.S. Geological Survey Water-Resources Investigations Report 02–4105, 60 p.

Daniel, C.C., III, and Payne, R.A., 1990, Hydrogeologic unit map of the Piedmont and Blue Ridge Provinces of North Carolina: U.S. Geological Survey Water-Resources Investigations Report 90–4035, 1 map sheet, scale 1:500,000.

Day-Lewis, F.D., White, E.A., Belaval, M., Johnson, C.D., and Lane, J.W., 2006, Continuous resistivity profiling to delineate submarine ground-water discharge—Examples and limitations: The Leading Edge. v. 25, no. 6, p. 724–728.

ENSR Consulting and Engineering, Inc., 2003, Supplemental site assessment report at the Neuse River Waste Water Treatment Plant, 108 p.

Fishman, M.J., ed., 1993, Methods of analysis by the U.S. Geological Survey National Water Quality Laboratory—Determination of inorganic and organic constituents in water and fluvial sediments: U.S. Geological Survey Open-File Report 93–125, 217 p.

Freeman, L.A., Carpenter, M.C., Rosenberry, D.O., Rousseau, J.P., Unger, R., and McLean, J.S., 2004, National field manual for the collection of hydrologic data—Use of submersible pressure transducers in water-resources investigations: U.S. Geological Survey Techniques of Water-Resources Investigations, book 8, chap. A3 [variously paged].

Garber, M.S., and Koopman, F.C., 1968, National field manual for the collection of hydrologic data—Methods of measuring water levels in deep wells: U.S. Geological Survey Techniques of Water-Resources Investigations, book 8, chap. A1 [variously paged].

Halford, K.J., and Kuniansky, E.L., 2002, Documentation of spreadsheets for the analysis of aquifer-test and slug-test data: U.S. Geological Survey Open-File Report 02–197, 54 p.

Harned, D.A., and Daniel, C.C., III, 1992, The transition zone between bedrock and saprolite-conduit for contamination? in Daniel, C.C., III, White, R.K., and Stone, P.A., eds., Ground water in the Piedmont of the Eastern United States: Clemson, SC, Clemson University, p. 336–348.

Heath, R.C., 1980, Basic elements of ground-water hydrology with reference to conditions in North Carolina: U.S. Geological Survey Open-File Report 80–44, 86 p.

Hibbard, J.P., Stoddard, E.F., Secor, D.T., and Dennis, A.J., 2002, The Carolina Zone, Overview of Neoproterozoic to early Paleozoic peri-Gondwanan terranes along the eastern flank of the southern Appalachians: Earth-Science Reviews, v. 57, no. 3, p. 299–339.

Keys, W.S., 1990, Borehole geophysics applied to ground-water investigations: U.S. Geological Survey Techniques of Water-Resources Investigations, book 2, chap. E2, 150 p.

LeGrand, H.E., 2004, A master conceptual model for hydro-geological site characterization in the Piedmont and Mountain region of North Carolina, A guidance manual: Raleigh, North Carolina Department of Environment and Natural Resources, Division of Water Quality, Groundwater Section, 50 p.

Munsell Soil Color Charts, 2000, revised washable edition: GretagMacbeth, 617 Little Britain Road, New Windsor, NY.

North Carolina Geological Survey, 1985, Geologic map of North Carolina. Raleigh, North Carolina Geological Survey, scale 1:500,000.

Piper, A.M., 1953, A graphic procedure in the geochemical interpretation of water analyses: Washington DC, U.S. Geological Survey, Ground-Water Chemistry Notes, no. 12, 14 p.

Rubin, Y., and Hubbard, S.S., eds., 2005, Hydrogeophysics: The Netherlands, Springer, 523 p.

Shapiro, A.M., 2001, Characterizing ground-water chemistry and hydraulic properties of fractured rock aquifers using the Multifunction Bedrock-Aquifer Transportable Testing Tool (Bat[3]): U.S. Geological Survey Fact Sheet FS–075–01, 4 p.

Sincich, T., 1993, Statistics by example: Upper Saddle River, New Jersey, Prentice Hall, p. 136–140.

Snyder, D.D., and Wightman, W.E., 2002, Application of continuous resistivity profiling to aqueous characterization, in Proceedings of the Symposium on the Application of Geophysics to Environmental and Engineering Problems (SAGEEP), February 10–14, 2002, Las Vegas, Nevada, Paper 13 GSL.

State Climate Office of North Carolina, 2007, Overview [of climate conditions in North Carolina]; accessed in September 2007 at *http://www.nc-climate.ncsu.edu/climate/ncclimate.html.*

Stiff, H.A., Jr., 1951, The interpretation of chemical water analysis by means of patterns: Journal of Petroleum Technology, v. 3, p. 15–17.

Taggart, J.E., Jr., ed., 2002, Analytical methods for chemical analysis of geologic and other materials, U.S. Geological Survey: U.S. Geological Survey Open-File Report 02–0223 [variously paged].

U.S. Geological Survey, 1974, Surface water supply of the United States, 1966–70, part 2. South Atlantic Slope and Eastern Gulf of Mexico Basins, v. 1, Basins from James River to Savannah River: U.S. Geological Survey Water-Supply Paper 2104, p. 3–10.

U.S. Geological Survey, 1975, Quality of surface water of the United States, 1970, part 3. Ohio River Basin: U.S. Geological Survey Water-Supply Paper 2153, p. 1–2.

U.S. Geological Survey, 1992, National Water Quality Laboratory Technical Memorandum 93–02; accessed in November 2008 at *http://nwql.usgs.gov/tech_memos/nwql.93-02.html.*

U.S. Geological Survey, 2006a, Collection of water samples (ver. 2.0): U.S. Geological Survey Techniques of Water-Resources Investigations, book 9, chap. A4, accessed February 20, 2008, at *http://pubs.water.usgs.gov/twri9A4/.*

U.S. Geological Survey, 2006b, Ground-water levels for North Carolina; accessed in January 2009 at *http://nwis.waterdata.usgs.gov/nc/nwis/gw/levels.*

U.S. Geological Survey, 2006c, USGS water data for North Carolina; accessed in January 2009 at *http://nwis.waterdata.usgs.gov/nc/nwis.*

U.S. Geological Survey, 2007, North Carolina water resources data report series, water-resources data, 2006; accessed in January 2009 at *http://nc.water.usgs.gov/reports/WDR/.*

U.S. Geological Survey, 2008, North Carolina water use data tables, 2005; accessed in January 2009 at *http://nc.water.usgs.gov/wateruse/data/Data_Tables_2005.html.*

Wagner, R.J., Boulger, R.W., Jr., Oblinger, C.J., and Smith, B.A., 2006, Guidelines and standard procedures for continuous water-quality monitors—Station operation, record computation, and data reporting: U.S. Geological Survey Techniques and Methods 1–D3 [variously paged].

Williams, J.H., and Conger, R.W., 1990, Preliminary delineation of contaminated water-bearing fractures intersected by open-borehole bedrock wells: Ground Water Monitoring Review, v. 10, no. 3, p. 118–126.

Appendixes

Appendix 1. Geologic core descriptions for WC-1CH from the Raleigh hydrogeologic research station

PROJECT: Raleigh hydrogeologic
BORING ID: WC-1CH
LOGGED BY: R. Bolich
COMPLETION DATE: 1/12/2005

DRILLING METHOD: wireline coring
CORE DIAMETER: 2.1 inches
Color descriptions referenced to Munsell soil color charts

SAMPLE INTERVAL (feet below land surface)			WATER BEARING UNIT	DESCRIPTION
0	to	1.1	ALLUVIUM	Mottled greyish brown (7.5 YR 5/3) silty fine to medium SAND abundant fine grained organic debris; moist.
1.1	to	3.6	ALLUVIUM	Reddish brown (10YR6/6) SILT; some fine sand trace clay; massive; slightly plastic.
3.6	to	8.6	ALLUVIUM	Light reddish/yellowish brown (7.5YR5/8) silty fine SAND; slightly mottled occasional mica flakes trace organic matter and/or Manganese stains; moist; friable.
8.6	to	12.5	ALLUVIUM	Yellowish brown FINE TO MEDIUM SAND little silt little coarse sand occasional mica trace organic matter; moist; loose.
12.5	to	14	ALLUVIUM	Yellowish brown and grey fine to coarse GRAVEL and COBBLES some medium to coarse sand trace silt; gravel and cobbles mostly quartz; subangular to well rounded; loose; moist.
14	to	33	ALLUVIUM & REGOLITH	Grey pink and white fine to coarse SAND little silt; sand is subangular quartz and feldspar; occasional biotite and/or vermiculite; moderate to well preserved relict granitic texture.
33	to	35	TRANSITION ZONE	Light grey and occasionally orange GRANITE; slightly weathered; contains biotite feldspar and quartz; mineral grain sizes range from medium to coarse; no fractures
35	to	40	TRANSITION ZONE	Light grey GRANITE; weathered to fresh; quartz filled fracture at 35.6 feet dips 30 degrees weathered near horizontal fractures at 36.0 36.3 36.5 and 36.6 feet.

PROJECT: Raleigh hydrogeologic
BORING ID: WC-1CH
LOGGED BY: R. Bolich
COMPLETION DATE: 1/12/2005

DRILLING METHOD: wireline coring
CORE DIAMETER: 2.1 inches
Color descriptions referenced to Munsell soil color charts

SAMPLE INTERVAL (feet below land surface)	WATER BEARING UNIT	DESCRIPTION
40 to 44	TRANSITION ZONE	Light grey GRANITE; slightly weathered;
44 to 46.5	BEDROCK	Pink and orange feldspar and biotite-rich PEGMATITE.
46.5 to 50	BEDROCK	Grey and pink GRANITE; slightly weathered to fresh - losing circulation @ 46 feet.
50 to 60	BEDROCK	Dark grey fine grained GRANITE.
60 to 64.7	BEDROCK	Grey and pink GRANITE; fresh; highly fractured;
64.7 to 75.8	BEDROCK	Grey and pink GRANITE; coarse grained; fresh.
75.8 to 78	BEDROCK	Grey GRANITE; fine grained.
78 to 89.5	BEDROCK	Grey and pink GRANITE; coarse grained; fresh.

Appendix 2. Geologic core descriptions for WC-2CH from the Raleigh hydrogeologic research station

PROJECT: Raleigh hydrogeologic
BORING ID: WC-2CH
LOGGED BY: R. Bolich
COMPLETION DATE: 2/8/2005

DRILLING METHOD: wireline coring
CORE DIAMETER: 2.1 inches
Color descriptions referenced to Munsell soil color charts

SAMPLE INTERVAL (feet below land surface)			WATER BEARING UNIT	DESCRIPTION
0	to	0.6	REGOLITH	Dark brown (2.5YR4/3) silty SAND and organic matter moist.
0.6	to	1.2	REGOLITH	Dark brown (2.5YR4/3) fine to medium SAND; little silt occasional organic matter and roots; moist.
1.2	to	7.3	REGOLITH	Reddish brown (2.5YR4/8) SILT; little to some fine to medium sand trace clay; mottled with darker brown organic rich sand with roots.
7.3	to	48	REGOLITH & TRANSITION ZONE	Yellowish grey (7.5YR7/3) fine to medium SAND; some silt; trace clay; poorly preserved rock fabric; moderately dense; moist.
48	to	50	TRANSITION ZONE	Pale olive (5Y6/3) clayey SILT; slightly plastic; stiff.
50	to	55	TRANSITION ZONE	Mottled dark reddish brown (2.5YR4/6) white and greenish grey silty CLAY and silty SAND; very poorly preserved structure; may be fault breccia saprolite; some moderately preserved granitic texture and some wavy laminated clayey silt oriented nearly vertical; granitic zones are loose and friable diabase saprolite is slightly plastic clayey silt.
55	to	60	TRANSITION ZONE	Olive grey (5Y5/2) and dark reddish brown (5YR3/4) clayey SILT; poorly preserved relict laminations nearly vertical orientation; stiff; slightly plastic; diabase saprolite with iron oxide fracture infills.
60	to	62	TRANSITION ZONE	Olive grey (5Y5/2) and dark reddish brown (5YR3/4) clayey SILT; poorly preserved relict laminations nearly vertical orientation; stiff; slightly plastic; diabase saprolite with iron oxide fracture infills.
62	to	64	TRANSITION ZONE	Dark grey slightly weathered DIABASE; highly fractured; some iron oxide and olive grey silt infills in fractures; random orientations and angles for fractures.

PROJECT: Raleigh hydrogeologic

BORING ID: WC-2CH

LOGGED BY: R. Bolich

COMPLETION DATE: 2/8/2005

DRILLING METHOD: wireline coring

CORE DIAMETER: 2.1 inches

Color descriptions referenced to Munsell soil color charts

SAMPLE INTERVAL (feet below land surface)			WATER BEARING UNIT	DESCRIPTION
64	to	70	TRANSITION ZONE	No Recovery
70	to	75	BEDROCK	Olive grey and dark reddish brown weathered DIABASE; recovered only 0.1 foot of five-foot long core.
75	to	80	BEDROCK	Light olive brown (2.5Y5/3) SILT mottled with dark reddish brown and light grey silt and sand; some clay; loose; friable; poorly preserved rock texture; sample appears to be diabase saprolite but may have some granitic saprolite "inclusions".
80	to	85	BEDROCK	Dark grey DIABASE; highly fractured but becoming fresh; dominant fractures/joints are nearly vertical; some blue mineralization (chlorite?) along vertical fractures.
85	to	90	BEDROCK	Weathered DIABASE; highly fractured; becoming more weathered with increasing depth; then transition at 86.4 feet to weathered GRANITE with abundant vertical fractures and iron oxide stains on fractures; weathering so pronounced that some of the rock is probably saprolite.
90	to	95	BEDROCK	Slightly weathered GRANITE; highly fractured; dominant fractures are nearly vertical; abundant iron oxide stains on all fractures.
95	to	100	BEDROCK	Highly fractured aphanitic pink-stained GRANITE (hornfels?); grading into silty sand and gravel granitic SAPROLITE.
100	to	105	BEDROCK	Highly weathered to slightly weathered GRANITE; becoming less fractured.
105	to	110	BEDROCK	Weathered coarse-grained GRANITE; moderately fractured; dominantly low-angle fractures.

Appendix 3. Geologic core descriptions for WC-3CH from the Raleigh hydrogeologic research station

PROJECT: Raleigh hydrogeologic
BORING ID: WC-3CH
LOGGED BY: R. Bolich
COMPLETION DATE: 12/14/2005

DRILLING METHOD: wireline coring
CORE DIAMETER: 2.1 inches
Color descriptions referenced to Munsell soil color charts

SAMPLE INTERVAL (feet below land surface)			WATER BEARING UNIT	DESCRIPTION
0	to	5	REGOLITH	Light yellowish brown silty fine to coarse SAND; some silt little clay; occasional vermiculite with some large (~2 cm) sheets; sand grains mostly quartz occasional feldspar; moderately preserved ganitic texture; loose; moist.
5	to	10	REGOLITH	Light yellowish brown to light grey fine to very coarse SAND; little silt trace vermiculite; very loose; moderately well preserved granitic texture; loosing most of sample due to high sand content; dry to slightly moist.
10	to	15	REGOLITH	Light yellowish brown fine to coarse SAND; some silt trace clay trace vermiculite and biotite; loose; friable; dry.
15	to	20	REGOLITH	Light yellowish and greyish brown fine to very coarse SAND; little fine to medium gravel little silt occasional vermiculite; moderately dense but loose and friable; well preserved granitic texture; moist.
20	to	25	REGOLITH	Light greyish brown fine to very coarse SAND; little silt trace fine to medium gravel occasional vermiculite; slightly dense; loose and friable; moderately well preserved granitic texture; slightly moist.
25	to	30	TRANSITION ZONE	Light yellowish brown grey and pink GRANITE; occasional vermiculite; dense; well preserved rock fabric; friable; moist;.
30	to	35	TRANSITION ZONE	Light greyish brown fine to coarse SAND; little silt trace clay occasional vermiculite; appears to be more weathered than previous sample; wet.
35	to	40	TRANSITION ZONE	White and light grey WEATHERED GRANITE; consists of quartz feldspar and biotite; slightly friable; exhibits some secondary porosity; iron-stained.
40	to	45	TRANSITION ZONE	Light grey GRANITE; slightly weathered; becomes less weathered after fracture at 40.4 feet.
45	to	50	TRANSITION ZONE	Light grey GRANITE; slightly weathered to highly weathered.

PROJECT: Raleigh hydrogeologic
BORING ID: WC-3CH
LOGGED BY: R. Bolich
COMPLETION DATE: 12/14/2005

DRILLING METHOD: wireline coring
CORE DIAMETER: 2.1 inches
Color descriptions referenced to Munsell soil color charts

SAMPLE INTERVAL (feet below land surface)			WATER BEARING UNIT	DESCRIPTION
50	to	55	TRANSITION ZONE	Highly weathered GRANITE and fine to very coarse SAND; sand is subangular quartz feldspar and fresh biotite; loose; poorly consolidated; coarse grained pegmatite from 53.2 to 55 feet
55	to	60	BEDROCK	Slightly weathered PEGMATITE and GRANITE; texture appears to be migmatitic; very coarse grained from 56.3 to 57.0 then aphanitic biotite granite from 57.0 to 58.0 then back to pegmatite dominated by pink feldspar from 58.0 - 59.0 feet.
60	to	64.5	BEDROCK	Fresh coarse grained biotite GRANITE;feldspar-rich interval from 64.5 - 64.7 feet.
64.5	to	70	BEDROCK	Fresh to slightly weathered biotite GRANITE;
70	to	75	BEDROCK	GRANITE: coarse grained fine grained mica feldspar quartz pyrite black white orange fresh.
75	to	80	BEDROCK	GRANITE: coarse grained fine grained mica feldspar quartz pyrite black white orange fresh.
80	to	85	BEDROCK	GRANITE: very coarse grained (PEGMATITE) feldspar mica quartz black white orange purple fresh.
85	to	90	BEDROCK	GRANITE: very coarse grained coarse grained (PEGMATITE) feldspar mica quartz black white orange pink slightly weathered fresh.
90	to	95	BEDROCK	GRANITE: very coarse grained (PEGMATITE) feldspar mica quartz black white orange pink slightly weathered fresh.
95	to	100	BEDROCK	GRANITE: fine grained coarse grained quartz feldspar mica fresh. slightly weathered.
100	to	105	BEDROCK	GRANITE: fine grained biotite feldspar and quartz; fresh to slightly weathered.
105	to	110	BEDROCK	GRANITE: fine grained biotite feldspar and quartz; slightly weathered.
110	to	115	BEDROCK	GRANITE: fine grained changing to coarse grained @ 111' feldspar quartz and biotite; pink and grey; fresh.
115	to	120	BEDROCK	GRANITE: coarse grained PEGMATITE vein from 118.8' to 119.1' feldspar quartz and biotite grey and pink fresh.

PROJECT: Raleigh hydrogeologic

BORING ID: WC-3CH

LOGGED BY: R. Bolich

COMPLETION DATE: 12/14/2005

DRILLING METHOD: wireline coring

CORE DIAMETER: 2.1 inches

Color descriptions referenced to Munsell soil color charts

SAMPLE INTERVAL (feet below land surface)	WATER BEARING UNIT	DESCRIPTION
120 to 125	BEDROCK	GRANITE: coarse grained feldspar quartz and biotite light grey pink and orange fresh.

Prepared by:
USGS Enterprise Publishing Network
Raleigh Publishing Service Center
3916 Sunset Ridge Road
Raleigh, NC 27607

For additional information regarding this publication, contact:
Kristen Bukowski McSwain
USGS North Carolina Water Science Center
3916 Sunset Ridge Road
Raleigh, NC 27607
phone: 919-571-4022
email: kmcswain@usgs.gov

Or visit the North Carolina Water Science Center Web site at:
http://nc.water.usgs.gov